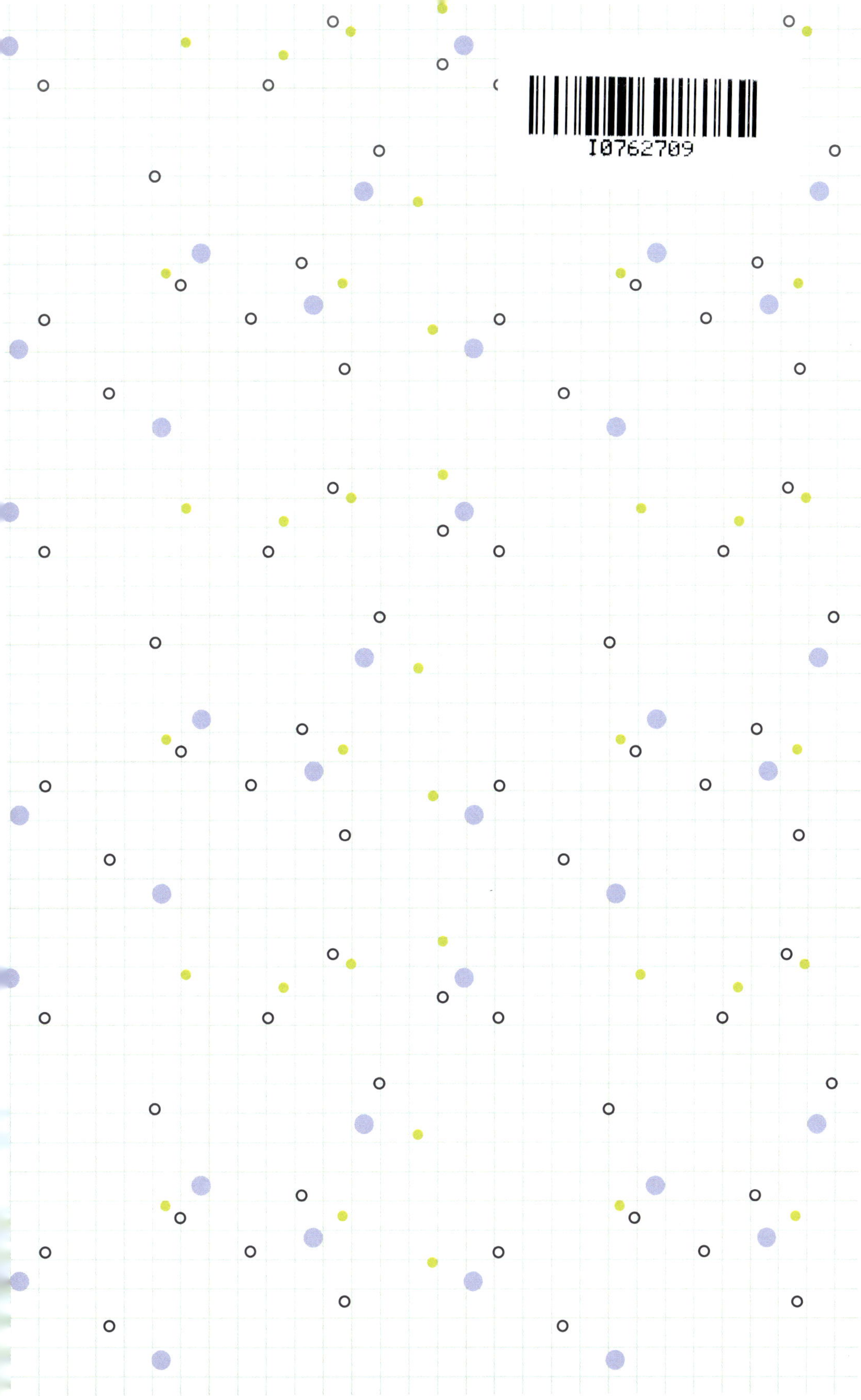
I0762709

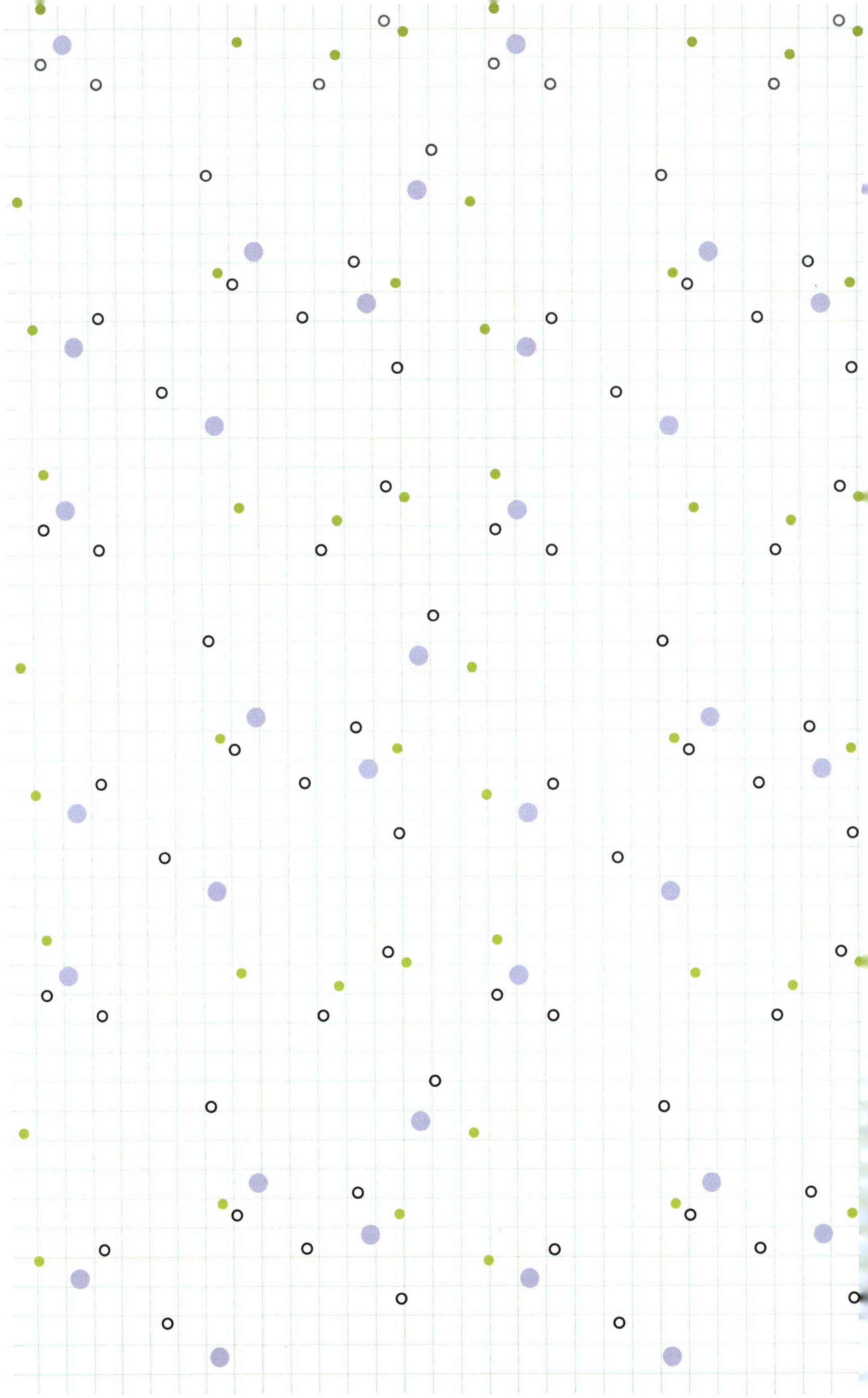

TO
FROM
DATE

Wow! I Didn't Know!

Things You Never Knew About the Stories of Jesus

DR. CRAIG EVANS
WITH GINNY EVANS

DaySpring
LIVE YOUR FAITH

First Edition, October 2025

Published by:

21154 Highway 16 East
Siloam Springs, AR 72761
dayspring.com

Written by: Dr. Craig Evans and Ginny Evans
Cover Design by: Lauren Purtle and Jon Huckeby

Printed in Vietnam
Prime: U3086
ISBN: 979-8-88602-926-0

Contents

Introduction

Welcome, readers. We are so glad you are here! Are you ready to be wowed? We are Craig and Ginny Evans, and we've been married and ministering together for over fifty years. Craig is a Bible scholar and professor, well-known for his work in the Gospels and New Testament manuscripts. And I, Ginny, am his trusty support staff. Craig is a prolific author, with much of his work designed for scholars and graduate students. However, he has always loved guiding non-scholars to a deeper understanding of the Bible and bringing it to life for them. To this end, it has long been in our hearts to write a book together so that we could share the "story behind the story" in an at-a-glance format with those who are intrigued by the background, context, and culture of Jesus and His disciples and want to dig deeper. Sound like fun? Let's get started.

The Bible is the world's best-selling book of all time. The best-known writings in the Bible are the Gospels, and the best-known human being of all time is Jesus of Nazareth. His life and ministry stand at the center of the Gospels. Yet, much of what Jesus said and did is often misunderstood. Why?

The main reason that the Bible, including the four Gospels, is difficult to interpret is because of its age. The many books that make up the Bible (which is why you should think of it as a small library) were written a long, long time ago and in languages that we don't speak. Also, the authors of the Bible's many books lived in a very different world when customs were unlike our own today.

We can read a passage in which Jesus said or did something and think we understand it. And most of the time we probably do understand the passage, or at least most of it. But often we don't know that we don't quite have it right. We miss some of the passage's meaning (and sometimes we might miss all of it!) because the story assumes knowledge of customs and current events that we moderns know nothing about.

We might also be unaware that the authors of the four Gospels were not writing in isolation, with no context and no purpose in mind other than simply telling the story of Jesus. On the contrary, the Gospels were written with very specific purposes in mind. The evangelist Matthew was deeply concerned to show that Jesus did not break the Law of Moses; He fulfilled it! The evangelist Mark was deeply concerned to show that Jesus was the true Son of God, the beginning of the good news for the world, not Caesar the Roman emperor. The evangelist Luke was deeply concerned to show that the good news of Jesus was for Gentiles, not just for the Jewish people. The evangelist John was deeply concerned to show that the death of Jesus fulfilled Scripture, and that His death on the cross did not nullify Jesus's mission but completed it.

Every passage in the Gospels needs to be carefully read in the light of the respective purposes of the four evangelists. But there is more: Each passage needs to be interpreted in the light of the customs and history of the time. When you read a parable about a great banquet, do you know that Jewish hopes for the appearance of the Messiah—when God would bless Israel and the world—were often referenced as a banquet? Or when you read about a wealthy man who lived in comfort, do you know that most of his contemporaries would have assumed that the man was chosen and on his way to heaven? Do you know that when Jesus stilled the storm, He did what Roman emperors wanted to do but couldn't? In the pages that follow, you will be treated to many more examples like this.

The goal of this little book is to make the riches of the Gospels more obvious and more understandable. And when these riches are better understood, you can more effectively learn how to apply their truths to your life and to be blessed by them. May this book be a gentle guide as you draw nearer to the heart of Jesus and discover the lasting joy found in His words.

Sincerely,

Dr. Craig Evans and Ginny Evans

Let the message about Christ, in all its richness, fill your lives.

COLOSSIANS 3:16 NLT

THE STORY OF

the Announcement of the Birth of Jesus

The Birth of Jesus

MAIN CHARACTERS

 **JOSEPH,** the husband of Mary and a descendant of David, was known in Nazareth as a carpenter or builder.

 **MARY,** a young virgin, also a native of Nazareth and a descendant of David, was chosen to be the mother of Jesus.

 **JESUS,** the principal figure in the Gospels and in the New Testament, is God's Son, and Israel's Messiah.

 **DAVID**, Israel's famous king, was the one whose lineage was destined to produce Israel's Messiah.

SCRIPTURE REFERENCE

Now in those days a decree went out from Caesar Augustus, that a census be taken of all the inhabited earth. This was the first census taken while Quirinius was governor of Syria. And everyone was on his way to register for the census, each to his own city. Joseph also went up from Galilee, from the city of Nazareth, to Judea, to the city of David which is called Bethlehem, because he was of the house and family of David, in order to register along with Mary, who was engaged to him, and was with child. While they were there, the days were completed for her to give birth. And she gave birth to her firstborn son; and she wrapped Him in cloths, and laid Him in a manger, because there was no room for them in the inn. (Luke 2:1–7)

What You Might Assume

Nazareth was an impoverished, isolated village.

The land of Israel was little more than a desert.

Joseph and Mary were poor and illiterate, and they seldom traveled.

Joseph and Mary were unable to find a room in the local inn. Jesus was born in a dirty barn.

Everyone expected the Messiah to come and fulfill prophecy.

Baby Jesus slept in a wooden feeding trough.

What Is More Likely

Nazareth was not isolated but was connected by well-traveled roads, with a major city only four miles away. Nazareth may have been founded by people from Bethlehem, many of whom were descendants of the family of King David, like Mary and Joseph's families.

Nazareth and Galilee as a whole were fertile and green and should not be confused with the Judean desert, as often portrayed in movies.

Joseph wasn't poor; rather, he likely possessed sufficient means to travel often to Jerusalem and nearby Bethlehem. Mary's family may not have been poor either. Both Joseph and Mary were descendants of King David and probably were respected in both Nazareth in Galilee and Bethlehem in Judea.

There was no room for Joseph and Mary in the guest room of the house where they stayed. They didn't stay in an inn, and their room was not a barn.

Many in Israel did not expect the coming of the Messiah; not all thought Old Testament prophecy would be fulfilled.

Feeding troughs in Jesus's day were typically made of stone.

The Story Behind the Scriptures

Every Christmas, Christians focus on the birth of Jesus. The beautiful stories of Matthew and Luke are reenacted. To fully appreciate this wonderful story, it is necessary to know something about the historical backdrop and context. The birth of Jesus didn't simply "come out of the blue."

Life was difficult for the Jewish people at the time of Jesus's birth. The hated and paranoid King Herod was near the end of his life. Would-be kings were recruiting followers, hoping to overthrow Rome and win freedom for Israel. Some didn't want change; they liked the way things were.

Although not all Jews in the first century expected a Messiah, many did. They believed that Isaiah's beautiful prophecy would someday be fulfilled: "For a child will be born to us, a son will be given to us; and the government will rest on His shoulders; And His name will be called Wonderful Counselor, Mighty God, Eternal Father, Prince of Peace" (Isaiah 9:6).

Those who clung to this reassuring prophecy assumed it would be fulfilled in some grand fashion. Surely this promised son—this descendant of David, Israel's greatest king—would come in glory and power, or so many assumed. But not so; He was born to humble parents, and He spent His first night in a feeding trough!

Let's take a closer look at the beloved yet often misrepresented nativity scene. It is true that the King James Version, as well as the New American Standard Bible, which is quoted on page 11, says that there was "no room for" Joseph and Mary "in the inn," but the Greek is better translated as "guest room." Mary and Joseph had likely gone to the home of friends or relatives, but their *guest room* (probably upstairs) already had another family in it. This is why Joseph and Mary were given the stable below (or beside) the house. But the stable is not outside in a barn; it is part of the house, downstairs, kind of like a modern garage. Mary and Joseph were afforded privacy, but we should assume that when Mary gave birth, she was assisted by family and friends.

Archaeology has uncovered the remains of the floors and foundations of some of these homes with connected stables. Archaeologists have also recovered mangers, or feeding troughs, which almost always were made of stone. The birth of Jesus and the first few days of his young life may have unfolded in a rustic setting, with animals nearby, but it was not in a dirty barn. And while we usually picture the three wise men visiting the infant Jesus, they didn't arrive until one or two years later.

The evangelist Matthew caught the significance of the birth of Jesus when he noted that it fulfilled yet another prophecy of Isaiah: "Behold, a virgin will be with child and bear a son, and she will call His name Immanuel," which means "God with us" (Isaiah 7:14 Author's Translation). In the birth of Jesus and in the fulfillment of this important prophecy, it would soon become clear that God was indeed with us, to save us from our sins (Matthew 1:21).

A KEY TAKEAWAY

God often chooses to use the least likely, the small, or the weak for His redemptive purposes. Here, the salvation of the world is seen in the birth of a child from a humble family, not from an influential family or in the arrival of a powerful army.

When Mary was told of her unexpected pregnancy, she responded, "May it be done to me according to your word" (Luke 1:38). She believed that the God of Israel could accomplish His purposes in her, a young woman of no power or influence. God can use us ordinary people for His purposes too. He has done it many times before, and He is still doing it today!

THE STORY OF

John's Recognition of Jesus

John's Recognition of Jesus

MAIN CHARACTERS

 **JOHN THE BAPTIST** was a popular preacher and prophet who baptized many Jews in the Jordan River.

 **JESUS** was one of John's early associates, who according to the Gospel of John, also baptized people who repented.

 **PRIESTS AND LEVITES,** clergy in ancient Israel, were all from the tribe of Levi. Priests were fully trained, while Levites were still in training.

 **PHARISEES,** religious leaders whose name may mean "Separated Ones," focused on keeping the Law of Moses perfectly.

 **ELIJAH** was a famous prophet whom many thought would return in the time of the Messiah.

SCRIPTURE REFERENCE

This is the testimony of John, when the Jews sent to him priests and Levites from Jerusalem to ask him, "Who are you?"

And he confessed and did not deny, but confessed, "I am not the Christ."

They asked him, "What then? Are you Elijah?" And he said, "I am not." "Are you the Prophet?" And he answered, "No."

Then they said to him, "Who are you, so that we may give an answer to those who sent us? What do you say about yourself?"

He said, "I am A VOICE OF ONE CRYING IN THE WILDERNESS, 'MAKE STRAIGHT THE WAY OF THE LORD,' as Isaiah the prophet said." . . .

"Why then are you baptizing, if you are not the Christ, nor Elijah, nor the Prophet?"

John answered . . . "I baptize in water, but among you stands One whom you do not know. It is He who comes after me, the thong of whose sandal I am not worthy to untie. . . . Behold, the Lamb of God who takes away the sin of the world! . . . I myself have seen, and have testified that this is the Son of God." (John 1:19–27, 29, 34)

What You Might Assume

Priests and Levites were sent from Jerusalem to check out John the Baptist's theology.

The statement that "Jews" sent the priests and Levites to John the Baptist sounds odd.

Definitions of "the Christ" and "the Prophet" were agreed upon by everyone.

Before the appearance of Jesus, no one claimed to be the Messiah; His claim was unique.

The Jordan River was little more than a muddy creek.

John the Baptist knew that Jesus was the Messiah.

What Is More Likely

Priests and Levites wanted to know more about John the Baptist's purpose and mission, not so much his theology.

In the Gospel of John, the term "Jews" is primarily a geographic designation, referring to the Jews who live in and around Jerusalem. They represent Israel's religious center. The Pharisees, who were the most influential, often confronted Jesus and His disciples with questions and criticisms.

Definitions of the Christ (or Messiah) and the expected Prophet differed widely; some people were so skeptical they didn't think the Messiah would ever appear.

There were many who claimed to be the Messiah and who claimed to be able to offer confirming signs.

The Jordan River was not a large river, but it was much more than a muddy creek.

John the Baptist learned for certain that Jesus was the Messiah when he baptized Him, saw the dove, and heard the heavenly voice.

The Story Behind the Scriptures

The story of John the Baptist in the Gospel of John tells us things that are not mentioned in the other three Gospels. The biggest difference is the way the story begins. The Jews sent priests and Levites from Jerusalem to ask John the Baptist, "Who are you?" We should assume that these "Jews" were not only Pharisees (mentioned in verse 24) but also ruling priests, including the high priest himself. An important part of their job was to keep an eye on things and to report potential trouble to the Roman governor. In the days of John the Baptist, the high priest was Caiaphas, and the Roman governor was Pontius Pilate. Both of these men will play important parts in the final days of Jesus.

What the Pharisees and other religious authorities wanted to know was what John the Baptist was telling the people. We know from other sources that the people loved John and hung on to his every word. What made the religious rulers especially nervous was that John was preaching and baptizing *at the Jordan River*, probably at the very spot where the people of Israel crossed the river and began their conquest of the Promised Land back in Old Testament times. John was not the only Israelite to preach in the wilderness in the first century. Others did too. For example, one man named Theudas urged the poor to follow him to the Jordan River, where he said God would miraculously part the water, just as He had done in the days of Joshua. The Romans attacked Theudas and his following, killing and imprisoning many.

No wonder "Jews from Jerusalem" wanted to know what John was up to. Was he the Messiah? Was he Elijah, expected at the end of days? Or was he the Prophet? If the former, was he Israel's promised king from the line of David? If one of the latter two, was he the prophet promised by Moses (Deuteronomy 18:15)? John said he wasn't any of these. His emphatic denials puzzled the religious authorities. If John wasn't the Messiah or Elijah, then who was he?

John's answer was just as puzzling. He said he was the "voice" calling out in the wilderness (an echo of Isaiah 40:3), preparing Israel for the greater One who would follow him. No one in the wilderness or at the River Jordan had ever said this before. All had pointed to themselves, promising to show the people signs of salvation. In contrast, John the Baptist spoke of one who would succeed him, whose sandal strap, he says, "I am not worthy to untie." And who was this successor? None other than the "Son of God." It was important to John to define his purpose and point to the true Messiah.

The priests and Levites would return to the religious authorities in Jerusalem with a startling report: John the Baptist himself was nothing special, no more than a "voice crying out in the wilderness" warning the people to prepare for the coming Son of God, the Lamb of God.

A KEY TAKEAWAY

John the Baptist was not just one more prophet among many. His message and baptizing were unique. He did not point to himself; he pointed to another, to the Son of God. But he did more than just talk; he saw for himself that Jesus was the Son of God, Israel's Messiah, and God's Lamb who would take away our sins. (In John 5:33 Jesus cites John as a key witness to His claims that He is the Son of God.)

The Baptism of Jesus

MAIN CHARACTERS

JOHN THE BAPTIST was a well-known prophet who preached repentance and baptized people in the Jordan River. One of his associates was Jesus of Nazareth.

JESUS, the principal character of the Gospel story, was related to John (their mothers were probably cousins). After His baptism and after John's arrest and imprisonment, Jesus began preaching.

THE SPIRIT OF GOD plays the starring role. He descends upon Jesus when Jesus comes up out of the water.

SCRIPTURE REFERENCE

Then Jesus arrived from Galilee at the Jordan coming to John, to be baptized by him. But John tried to prevent Him, saying, "I have need to be baptized by You, and do You come to me?" But Jesus answering said to him, "Permit it at this time; for in this way it is fitting for us to fulfill all righteousness." Then he permitted Him. After being baptized, Jesus came up immediately from the water; and behold, the heavens were opened, and he saw the Spirit of God descending as a dove and lighting on Him, and behold, a voice out of the heavens said, "This is My beloved Son, in whom I am well-pleased." (Matthew 3:13–17)

In those days Jesus came from Nazareth in Galilee and was baptized by John in the Jordan. Immediately coming up out of the water, He saw the heavens opening, and the Spirit like a dove descending upon Him; and a voice came out of the heavens: "You are My beloved Son, in You I am well-pleased." (Mark 1:9–11)

Now when all the people were baptized, Jesus was also baptized, and while He was praying, heaven was opened, and the Holy Spirit descended upon Him in bodily form like a dove, and a voice came out of heaven, "You are My beloved Son, in You I am well-pleased." (Luke 3:21–22)

What You Might Assume

Jesus did not need to repent, so He really didn't need to be baptized. This is why John (in the Gospel of Matthew) initially tries to prevent Jesus from being baptized.

"Coming up out of the water" means Jesus going up from the river back onto the shore.

When the Holy Spirit descended on Jesus "like a dove," He received the Spirit for the first time and was ready for ministry.

Only Jesus heard the voice from the heavens.

What Is More Likely

Jesus went to be baptized, not because he needed to confess His sins but because He fully embraced John's message. In doing so, Jesus sets the right example, or, as Jesus says in Matthew, "It is fitting for us to fulfill all righteousness." That is, Jesus's conduct is *right*.

"Coming up out of the water" means Jesus had been fully immersed (the literal meaning of *baptism*). Accordingly, Jesus emerged from the water, but He was still in the Jordan River.

At the moment of emerging from the water, Jesus saw heaven open and the Spirit of God descending on Him "like a dove." This was not the first time Jesus had received the Spirit. Jesus was conceived by the Holy Spirit (Luke 1:35).

The versions of the story in Mark and Luke do give the impression that the words of the heavenly voice, "You are My beloved Son," were only heard by Jesus. It is probable, however, that John also, and perhaps others, heard the heavenly voice. If so, this would explain why the words appear slightly differently in Matthew's version of the story: "This is My beloved Son."

The Story Behind the Scriptures

In churches today, baptism is practiced in a variety of ways. Although the Greek word *baptism* literally means "immersion," some churches baptize believers by sprinkling or pouring. In the time of John and Jesus, however, baptism was literal immersion. The apostle Paul even compared baptism with burial (see Colossians 2:12), which only makes sense if the word *baptism* means "to be immersed."

So, where did the idea of water immersion come from? It began with Moses, who commanded that when the priests enter the tabernacle (what, in time, would become the temple), "they shall wash them with water" (Exodus 30:20; 40:12). To safeguard purity, Moses provided instructions with regard to washing clothes and bathing in water (Leviticus 15–17).

In the time of John and Jesus, most synagogues had ritual immersion pools where people could immerse themselves before entering the building. Archaeologists have uncovered many of these pools in Jerusalem, including several around the Temple Mount. Many Jewish homes, including homes in Galilee, had ritual immersion pools. Of course, the most symbolic, if not most sacred, place for immersion was the Jordan River, which is where John did most of his baptizing. Being baptized in the Jordan not only signified ritual purity; it was also a reminder of Joshua crossing the river to claim the Promised Land.

What strikes us as especially interesting is the way Luke describes the descent of the dove. Both Matthew and Mark say the Spirit descended on Jesus "like a dove," but Luke says that it was while Jesus "was praying" that "the Holy Spirit descended upon Him in bodily form like a dove." In the book of Acts, we often read of prayer. We also see the connection between prayer and the pouring out of the Holy Spirit. On one occasion the followers of Jesus are filled with the Holy Spirit, and the building itself is shaken (Acts 4:31). That seems to be what Luke is saying in the baptism of Jesus. After Jesus emerged from the water, He prayed, and then the Holy Spirit descended on Him *bodily* (which is what the

Greek text literally says). That is, the Holy Spirit came upon Jesus not as a mere symbol or metaphor ("like a dove") but as a powerful substance, something tangible, something to shake things up. And that is exactly what happened—the ministry of Jesus shook the world.

KEY TAKEAWAY

The baptism of Jesus was much more than a religious act or symbol. It was a powerful, dynamic catalyst that launched the ministry of Jesus. The baptism of Jesus resulted in an unprecedented empowerment of God's Holy Spirit that carried Jesus through his ministry, to the cross, to His resurrection, and into heaven itself. That same Holy Spirit is available to us and is more than able to shake things up.

THE STORY OF

the Temptation of Jesus

The Temptation of Jesus

MAIN CHARACTERS

JESUS, the principal figure in the New Testament Gospels, was baptized by John and then led into the wilderness to be tempted by Satan.

SATAN, archenemy of God and humankind, is traditionally believed to be a fallen high-ranking angel.

ANGELS, known as "messengers," serve God and often speak to or minister to human beings.

SCRIPTURE REFERENCE

Then Jesus was led up by the Spirit into the wilderness to be tempted by the devil. And after He had fasted forty days and forty nights, He then became hungry. And the tempter came and said to Him, "If You are the Son of God, command that these stones become bread." But He answered and said, "It is written, 'MAN SHALL NOT LIVE ON BREAD ALONE, BUT ON EVERY WORD THAT PROCEEDS OUT OF THE MOUTH OF GOD.'"

Then the devil took Him into the holy city and had Him stand on the pinnacle of the temple, and said to Him, "If You are the Son of God, throw Yourself down; for it is written,
'HE WILL COMMAND HIS ANGELS CONCERTING YOU';
and
'ON THEIR HANDS THEY WILL BEAR YOU UP,
SO THAT YOU WILL NOT STRIKE YOUR FOOT AGAINST A STONE.'"

Jesus said to him, "On the other hand, it is written, 'YOU SHALL NOT PUT THE LORD YOUR GOD TO THE TEST.'"

Again, the devil took Him to a very high mountain and showed Him all the kingdoms of the world and their glory; and he said to Him, "All these things I will give You, if You fall down and worship me." Then Jesus said to him, "Go, Satan! For it is written, 'YOU SHALL WORSHIP THE LORD YOUR GOD, AND SERVE HIM ONLY.'" Then the devil left Him; and behold, angels came and began to minister to Him. (Matthew 4:1–11)

What You Might Assume

God sent Jesus to be tempted by Satan.

Jesus was tempted in a desert.

Jesus did not eat or drink for forty days.

The temptations did not take place in real time but were no more than dreams or thoughts.

What Is More Likely

!

Jesus was "led by the spirit" to go into the wilderness to meditate and find resolve. The word *tempted* can also be understood as *tested.*

The word *wilderness* refers to an uninhabited area, not to a desert.

Fasting does not necessarily refer to total abstinence from food and drink. Rather, fasting usually meant a much-reduced intake of food and no wine, but one always drank water.

The temptations were quite real and did take place in real time, though one or two of them may have involved visions.

The Story Behind the Scriptures

We have all experienced temptations; they can pop up in an instant and without warning. The most dangerous of temptations is the shortcut to get what we want (which might be a good and noble thing). But taking the shortcut is going about it the wrong way. That was the essence of the temptations that Jesus faced. But Jesus wasn't the first to be tempted by Satan.

Satan tempted Adam and Eve. The point of the temptation was not simply to persuade them to ignore God's command by eating fruit from the forbidden tree. The temptation was to take a shortcut, to get to "the knowledge of good and evil" quickly, to become like God. Alas, Adam and Eve took the bait and fell.

Well, Satan was at it again. He had tricked Adam and Eve by tempting them with food. Maybe he could do it again with Jesus. How strong was Jesus's commitment to God? Could Jesus pass the test? Was Jesus the real deal?

Our story begins after Jesus had been fasting for a month and was seriously hungry. But Satan didn't just offer Jesus food; he suggested that Jesus demonstrate His authority by commanding stones to become bread—something Moses in the wilderness could have only dreamed of doing!

Jesus recognized the temptation for what it was—to follow Satan rather than God, to take a shortcut to get what He needed right then. But Jesus refused, quoting Deuteronomy 8:3 (NKJV), "Man shall not live by bread alone." This is one of the very lessons that the Israelites missed when they were in the wilderness, grumbling for food.

Satan tried again, this time suggesting that Jesus demonstrate his faith that God would send his angels to protect Him. And Jesus replied with a quotation from Deuteronomy 6:16 (NKJV), "You shall not tempt the LORD your God."

Satan tried one more time, showing Jesus the whole world and offering it to Him, if Jesus would just fall down and worship him. Isn't this what Jesus wanted—the whole world? After His resurrection, did He not command His apostles to go out into the world and make disciples of all nations (Matthew 28:18–20)? In effect, Satan has once again offered Jesus a shortcut, and once again Jesus refuses, replying with a quotation from Deuteronomy 6:13 (NIV), "Fear the Lord your God, serve Him only."

In His ministry, Jesus would do all three things that the three temptations assumed He could do: He exercised authority (in miracles); He demonstrated faith in God (in going to the cross); and He claimed the nations for Himself (in sending his apostles into the world). Yet, at the heart of the three temptations was corruption and sin. In these three areas, Israel had failed miserably in their wilderness wanderings. Moses warned the second generation of Israelites, about to cross the Jordan and enter the Promised Land, not to succumb to these temptations. Jesus, the faithful Israelite, obeyed the commands of Scripture (and this is why Jesus replied with three citations from the book of Deuteronomy). He would accomplish all that the temptations promised, but He would do them God's way, not Satan's way.

KEY TAKEAWAY

The objects of temptations are not always wrong. Many of them are centered on good things. But it's how we get there that is often the problem. And the problem at the heart of the temptation is often a shortcut. Wanting a good grade is not bad, but cheating to get it is. There are many things in life that we need and many that we desire. It is not wrong to need them and to desire them, but dishonoring God or harming a neighbor is not the way. Jesus models for us the right response to temptation—and that response is to stay focused on His will as expressed in Scripture.

THE STORY OF

Jesus Turning Water into Wine

Jesus Turns Water into Wine

MAIN CHARACTERS

JESUS THE SON OF GOD (AND SON OF MARY) is the principal figure in the four Gospels and throughout New Testament.

MARY, the mother of Jesus, appears throughout the Gospels as a devoted and faithful figure.

THE HEADWAITER was the man in charge of the refreshments at the wedding feast.

THE DISCIPLES OF JESUS, whose training under Jesus has just begun, were at the early stages of their journey with Him.

SCRIPTURE REFERENCE

On the third day there was a wedding in Cana of Galilee, and the mother of Jesus was there; and both Jesus and His disciples were invited to the wedding. When the wine ran out, the mother of Jesus said to Him, "They have no wine." And Jesus said to her, "Woman, what does that have to do with us? My hour has not yet come." His mother said to the servants, "Whatever He says to you, do it."

Now there were six stone waterpots set there for the Jewish custom of purification, containing twenty or thirty gallons each. Jesus said to them, "Fill the waterpots with water." So they filled them up to the brim. And He said to them, "Draw some out now and take it to the headwaiter." So they took it to him.

When the headwaiter tasted the water which had become wine, and did not know where it came from (but the servants who had drawn the water knew), the headwaiter called the bridegroom, and said to him, "Every man serves the good wine first, and when the people have drunk freely, then he serves the poorer wine; but you have kept the good wine until now."

This beginning of His signs Jesus did in Cana of Galilee, and manifested His glory, and His disciples believed in Him. (John 2:1–11)

What You Might Assume

?

Only one couple was getting married.

Mary knew the hosts personally, and she didn't want her friends to be embarrassed, which is why she stepped in

It seems that Jesus made far more wine than needed.

Jesus didn't make wine; perhaps it was only grape juice.

Jesus seemed to respond harshly and disrespectfully to His mother.

What Is More Likely

!

The wedding feast may have been in honor of two or three couples.

Mary was probably the hostess.

Perhaps Jesus made the exact amount of wine that was needed.

Jesus made real wine; otherwise, the steward's comment in verse 10 doesn't make sense.

Jesus did not show His mother disrespect; He took advantage of a teaching moment.

The Story Behind the Scriptures

Jewish weddings often took place during the Feast of Purim, or the Festival of Lights, when wine flowed freely. It was a Jewish holiday celebrating the deliverance of the Jewish people from a plot to exterminate them, as described in the Book of Esther. Combining weddings with the celebration of Purim was a good way to hold several expensive events at once and would, of course, explain why so much wine was needed.

Mary, the mother of Jesus, was probably the hostess, which explains her role in the story. She informed her Son that the wine had run out. But why did Jesus address His mother so abruptly with the word, "Woman"? Was Jesus disrespectful? Not in the least! In the culture of the day, this is how women were addressed. Indeed, while on the cross Jesus addressed His mother this way with affection (John 19:26). When Jesus asked, "What does that have to do with us," He was asking why the lack of wine should concern Him. After all, the wine that really counts will come into play at the Last Supper, when Jesus instructs His disciples that the wine of Passover symbolizes His blood. It will be in His death and the shedding of His blood that His "hour" of glorification will arrive.

Mary rightly understood what her Son was saying, and so she instructed the servants, "Whatever He says to you, do it." Jesus told the servants to fill the water jars to the brim and then take a cup to the headwaiter. When the headwaiter tasted the water—which is now wine—he exclaimed, "You have kept the good wine until now." The wine Jesus made was excellent, better than the wine served at the beginning of the wedding celebration. Please understand, Jesus is talking about real wine, not grape juice!

Jesus not only astonished people when He turned the water into wine, but the significance of the miracle would also have brought to mind a variety of thoughts to those who saw or heard of it. The miracle would have made some think of the pagan god Dionysius, son of Zeus (the highest of the pagan gods). This may surprise you, but pagan myths were well-known even in Israel. The story is told of Dionysius, who thanked a kind farmer by turning water into wine. The farmer was astonished at the purple water's taste. In telling the story of Jesus changing water into wine, John pushed back against the Greek myths of the day to show that Jesus is truly God and can provide for human needs, even as Moses provided water and bread in the wilderness (Exodus 16:4–22; 17:1–6).

In changing water into wine—and a lot of it at that!—Jesus demonstrated His glory. This is a very important point because the Jewish people believed that only God possessed glory. Now they've heard that Jesus possesses glory too. Turning the water into wine was the first of seven major signs. In the signs to come, Jesus will demonstrate His glory again and again.

KEY TAKEAWAY

In this very important miracle, the first of Jesus's "signs," the evangelist John has shown how Jesus begins to make known His glory, a glory that will reach its most important point when Jesus goes to the cross, sheds His blood, and makes salvation possible for all of us.

THE STORY OF
the Beginning of
Jerusalem

Jesus Calls for Repentance

MAIN CHARACTERS

JOHN THE BAPTIST, a colleague of Jesus, was imprisoned by Herod Antipas, one of the the rulers of Galilee. John urged the people of Israel to repent.

JESUS is the central figure in this passage and throughout the New Testament Gospels. Like His predecessor John, He called Israel to repent and believe the good news of the kingdom of God. After John's imprisonment by Herod Antipas, Jesus began His ministry from Capernaum, on the Northwest Shore of the Sea of Galilee.

ISAIAH THE PROPHET lived in the eighth century BC. His prophecies often referred to Israel's Messiah.

KEY LOCATIONS are Galilee, the northern region of Israel where much of Jesus's ministry occurred; Nazareth, His hometown; Capernaum, His base on the Sea of Galilee's northwest shore; and Zebulun and Naphtali, ancestral territories named after Israelite patriarchs whose descendants settled in Galilee.

SCRIPTURE REFERENCE

Now when Jesus heard that John had been taken into custody, He withdrew into Galilee; and leaving Nazareth, He came and settled in Capernaum . . . in the region of Zebulun and Naphtali. This was to fulfill what was spoken through Isaiah the prophet:

"THE LAND OF ZEBULUN AND . . . NAPHTALI,
BY THE WAY OF THE SEA ... GALILEE OF THE GENTILES—
"THE PEOPLE . . . SITTING IN DARKNESS SAW A GREAT LIGHT,
AND THOSE . . . IN THE LAND AND SHADOW OF DEATH,
UPON THEM A LIGHT DAWNED."

From that time Jesus began to preach and say, "Repent, for the kingdom of heaven is at hand." (Matthew 4:12–17)

What You Might Assume

The kingdom was something physical—like the overthrowing of Rome and the restoration of the kingdom of Israel on Earth.

The kingdom of heaven and the kingdom of God are two different things, one perhaps referring to heaven above and the other to the earth below.

The original "good news" that Jesus preached was telling people to believe in Him (perhaps in the sense of becoming a Christian and joining a local church).

The expression "Galilee of the Gentiles" implies that the land of Galilee in Jesus's time had a significant Gentile presence, possibly indicating a smaller or more dispersed Jewish population.

The call to repentance meant the world was about to end.

What Is More Likely

It is true that some people in Israel expected that Rome would be overthrown when the kingdom of God arrived.

The expressions "kingdom of heaven" and "kingdom of God" are one and the same; they are not referring to two different things. Because of Jewish sensitivities regarding referring to God, sometimes substitutes like "heaven" were used.

When Jesus proclaimed the "good news," or gospel, He was referring to the rule of God on earth. The same idea is expressed in the Lord's Prayer, where Jesus petitions God that His "kingdom come" and His "will be done" *on earth as it is in heaven* (Matthew 6:10). Originally, the good news that Jesus proclaimed did not center on Himself. After the resurrection of Jesus, the good news that the Church proclaimed was that Jesus was raised up, that forgiveness in His name was possible, and that the kingdom of God was still very much on its way.

Galilee was called "Galilee of the Gentiles" in Isaiah's famous prophecy. Matthew quotes the prophecy, not because Galilee was populated by Gentiles but because Jewish Galilee was surrounded to the west, north, and east by Gentiles. The words of the prophecy may also have hinted at the Church's mission, in which the risen Jesus commands His apostles to preach the good news to and make disciples of all the nations—the Gentiles (Matthew 28:18–20).

The call to repentance had nothing to do with the end of the world but the beginning of the world's renewal.

The Story Behind the Scriptures

When we hear of "repentance," we often think of a crazy street prophet warning of coming doom: "Repent! Judgment is at hand!" Usually, this "judgment" is understood as the end of the world, either through war or natural disasters (and Hollywood loves making disaster movies). But that is rarely what the call to repentance means in the Bible.

In the Bible, calls for repentance are almost always calls for moral and spiritual renewal. They are urgent appeals to come back to God and to seek restoration. When King Solomon dedicated the temple in Jerusalem, he prayed that if the people of Israel were ever taken captive, they would repent and make supplication to God so that they may be forgiven and restored (I Kings 8:46–48). Two centuries later, the prophet Isaiah reminded sinful Israel, "In repentance and rest you will be saved" (Isaiah 30:15). Unfortunately, a century later, when Babylon threatened Jerusalem, the people "refused to repent" (Jeremiah 5:3; 8:6; 15:7), and calamity overtook them.

The words *repent* and *repentance* can and sometimes do mean "to change one's mind, to rethink," as it were. But in the Bible, *repent* and *repentance* usually mean "to return, to come back, to get back on the path that leads to God and obedience." This is beautifully illustrated in the parable of the prodigal son (Luke 15, which will be discussed later in this book). The young son foolishly leaves his family and journeys to a foreign land, where he becomes ensnared in sin and hardship, but when he comes to his senses (and here *repentance* in the sense of changing his mind is implied), he *returns* home, and fellowship is restored. The young man has returned to his faith, and now the brokenness of his family can begin to heal.

Let's pursue the idea of restoration further. Restoration is a very important dimension of repentance. Repentance isn't just saying, "I'm sorry;" it is a life-altering change of the person, of the whole person. The world is no longer seen the same way. How we see ourselves and how we see others are no longer the same. God is no longer seen the same way. God is no longer seen as a celestial Santa Claus who gives us whatever we request, or an angry, unloving ogre who is never satisfied. God is seen as He really is—holy, loving, and merciful. Repentance opens the door of salvation, or for those already saved, repentance restores the soul and brings one back into healthy fellowship with God and with other believers.

KEY TAKEAWAY

Jesus's call for repentance was a vital part of his proclamation of the good news of God's kingdom. To embrace this good news, to be blessed by the refreshing and restorative power of God's kingdom, it is necessary to repent. For those who are already God's children, repentance cleans the heart, "takes out the trash," restores the soul, and permits the renewing sunshine of God's grace to flood back into our lives.

THE STORY OF

Jesus Preaching at Nazareth

Jesus Declares Isaiah's Prophecy Fulfilled and Good News for All

MAIN CHARACTERS

 **JESUS,** the principal figure in the Gospels and the New Testament, returned to His hometown and synagogue, where He preached to a keenly interested crowd.

 **NAZARETH** was the small village in Galilee where Jesus grew up. Archaeology has shown that though small, in the time of Jesus the village was bustling with activity.

 **ISAIAH** is likely Jesus's favorite book of Scripture, which He read and preached about in the Nazareth synagogue.

 **THE PEOPLE OF NAZARETH,** many of whom were acquaintances of Jesus, were in attendance at the synagogue when Jesus spoke.

SCRIPTURE REFERENCE

And He came to Nazareth, where He had been brought up; and as was His custom, He entered the synagogue on the Sabbath, and stood up to read. And the book of the prophet Isaiah was handed to Him . . .

"THE SPIRIT OF THE LORD IS UPON ME,
BECAUSE HE ANOINTED ME TO PREACH THE GOSPEL TO THE POOR.
HE HAS SENT ME TO PROCLAIM RELEASE TO THE CAPTIVES,
AND RECOVERY OF SIGHT TO THE BLIND,
TO SET FREE THOSE WHO ARE OPPRESSED, TO
PROCLAIM THE FAVORABLE YEAR OF THE LORD."

And He closed the book, gave it back to the attendant and sat down . . . "Today this Scripture has been fulfilled in your hearing." . . . They were saying, "Is this not Joseph's son?" And He said to them, "No doubt you will quote this proverb to Me, 'Physician, heal yourself! . . . [And] do here in your hometown as well.'" . . . "There were many widows in Israel in the days of Elijah . . . yet Elijah was sent . . . to a woman who was a widow." "And there were many lepers in Israel in the time of Elisha . . . none . . . was cleansed, but only Naaman the Syrian." . . . They got up and drove Him out . . . to throw Him down the cliff. But passing through their midst, He went His way. (Luke 4:16–30)

What You Might Assume

It was presumptuous for Jesus to preach in the synagogue. After all, He had not been formally ordained.

It was presumptuous for Jesus to claim that the prophecy of Isaiah was being fulfilled in His ministry.

The reference to Joseph was intended to belittle Jesus, perhaps implying that He was of no special importance.

The reference to the saying, "Physician, heal yourself," implied that there was something wrong with Jesus.

The negative reactions to the references to Elijah and Elisha were because these prophets were unpopular in Nazareth.

The attempt to throw Jesus over the cliff failed because of a miracle.

What Is More Likely

It was not at all presumptuous for Jesus to preach in the Nazareth synagogue. Jesus had become well-known—and popular—as a preacher who often spoke in the synagogues in Galilee. A respected man was called "rabbi," but there was no formal ordination, or any formal ceremony in which He was set apart to lead others.

It was not presumptuous for Jesus to claim that the prophecy of Isaiah was being fulfilled in His ministry. Jesus (and John the Baptist before Him) had already appealed to Isaiah, and no one had objected. In Luke 4:22, the people wondered "at the gracious words which were falling from His lips." The quotation of Isaiah and the claim that it was fulfilled were well received by the synagogue congregation.

The reference to Joseph does not appear to be negative at all. It was to identify Jesus, who had been away for some time.

The saying, "Physician, heal yourself," was a well-known proverb. It didn't necessarily imply that the one claiming to be a physician was ill. In the context of the story above, the meaning is clear: Jesus is expected to give priority to the people of Nazareth—His family and neighbors—even more than He has to people of other towns, such as Capernaum.

The negative reactions to the references to Elijah and Elisha were due to Jesus's application of these stories. Galileans were proud that these prophets had ministered in Galilee long ago.

The attempt to throw Jesus over the cliff failed not because of a miracle (and there is no hint that a miracle occurred) but because the anger of the crowd dissipated, and Jesus, with authority, pushed His way through it and left town.

The Story Behind the Scriptures

Before Jesus arrived in Nazareth, His hometown, to preach, He had been preaching in synagogues "and was praised by all" (Luke 4:15). So what went wrong at Nazareth? The problem was the assumption that the wonderful blessings foretold by Isaiah the prophet were, first and foremost, intended for the people of Israel. It was further assumed that because Jesus was himself from Nazareth, the people of Nazareth should receive the lion's share of these blessings. The people in the synagogue were probably miffed that Jesus had already blessed the people of Capernaum and other villages of Galilee. They may have wondered, "Why is Jesus just now getting around to us?" The people of Nazareth expected exclusive privileges. In today's world, it would be like a local man elected to high office. The locals expect some benefits to come their way! But that wasn't Jesus's plan.

All were happy when Jesus quoted Isaiah and said His prophecy was fulfilled in their hearing. But when Jesus appealed to the well-known stories of Elijah and Elisha, He lost His listeners. Why? Because these two prophets ministered to Gentiles! Elijah ministered to a poor, starving Gentile widow and her young son (see I Kings 17:1–16). The people of Nazareth might have been willing to overlook that, but when Jesus referred to Elisha, who ministered to Namaan, the captain in the Syrian army, a fierce enemy of Israel (see II Kings 5:1–14), that was too much! The people of Nazareth rightly understood that Jesus was suggesting that the messianic blessings promised in Isaiah would be extended not only to Gentiles but even to Gentiles who oppressed Israel! Let's not forget that much of Israel in the time of Jesus was under the Roman thumb. Was Jesus implying that the Messiah's blessings would benefit the Romans as well as Israel?

The grace of God that Jesus envisioned was simply too difficult to grasp.

KEY TAKEAWAY

The story of Jesus's preaching in Nazareth and the angry response to it teaches us a great lesson. It is all too tempting to think that God's mercies and blessings belong to us—and not to others. Surely, God will bless us much more than He will bless strangers, and certainly much more than people we regard as enemies. Jesus teaches that God wishes to bless all—us and everybody else. A big part of the good news is how big it is.

THE STORY OF

Jesus Calling the Disciples

Jesus Calls Fishermen to Be His Disciples

MAIN CHARACTERS

JESUS, the central figure of the Gospels and the New Testament, was known as a builder before His public ministry—not a fisherman, which makes this chapter's story all the more striking.

A CROWD gathered around Jesus to hear His teaching. Crowds often followed Him, sometimes making it hard for Him to find quiet or rest.

SIMON PETER—originally named Simon and later called Peter ("Rock") by Jesus after confessing Him as Messiah (Matt. 16)—was a professional fisherman.

JAMES AND JOHN, sons of Zebedee, were fellow fishermen and acquaintances of Simon Peter and his brother Andrew.

SCRIPTURE REFERENCE

Now it happened that while the crowd was pressing around Him and listening to the word of God, He was standing by the lake of Gennesaret; and He saw two boats . . . but the fishermen had gotten out . . . and were washing their nets. And He got into one of the boats, which was Simon's, and asked him to put out a little way from the land. And He sat down and began teaching the people from the boat. When He had finished, He said to Simon, "Put out into the deep water and let down your nets for a catch." Simon answered . . . "Master, we worked hard all night and caught nothing, but I will do as You say . . ." When they had done this, they enclosed a great quantity of fish, and their nets began to break; so they signaled . . . the other boat . . . and they came and filled both . . . boats, so that they began to sink. But when Simon Peter saw that, he fell down at Jesus's feet, saying, "Go away from me, Lord, for I am a sinful man!" For amazement had seized him and all his companions . . . and so also were James and John, sons of Zebedee, who were partners with Simon. And Jesus said to Simon, "Do not fear, from now on you will be catching men." When they had brought their boats to land, they left everything and followed Him. (Luke 5:1–11)

What You Might Assume

?

The crowd listening to Jesus was primarily interested in Jesus's teaching, less so the miracles.

The fishermen Simon Peter and his friends were poor because fishing provided a meager income. Surprisingly, Jesus selected such ordinary men as these.

Simon Peter and his friends may not have been very good at catching fish, as the story of the miraculous catch of fish may presuppose.

Leaving their boats to follow Jesus did not amount to much of a sacrifice.

What Is More Likely

The crowds surrounding Jesus were as much concerned with healing as they were with Jesus's teaching. In fact, on one occasion, Jesus accuses the crowd of coming to Him that they might be fed (John 6:26).

Simon Peter and his fishermen brother and friends probably made a good living; they were not wealthy, but they were not poor either. Indeed, we are told that Zebedee, the father of James and John, had servants and possibly more than one boat (Mark 1:20). These men were resourceful and resilient. It is not surprising that Jesus chose them to be His disciples.

Simon Peter's lack of success fishing on this particular occasion was the result of bad luck, not incompetence. Of course, his failure to enjoy a successful night of fishing set the stage for the miraculous catch of fish later in the day.

Leaving their boats represented a major sacrifice. Their boats would have been very expensive to build and would have been valued not only for fishing but also for ferrying people and goods. Simon Peter, on a later occasion, complained to Jesus, "Behold, we have left everything and followed You" (Mark 10:28). Leaving behind their boats and other possessions represented a serious loss of property and income.

The Story Behind the Scriptures

We are told that "the crowd was pressing around" Jesus (Luke 5:1). In reading the Gospels, one gets the impression that everywhere Jesus went, crowds followed (e.g., Matthew 4:25; 8:1). So why did crowds follow Jesus? To be sure, they wanted to listen to Jesus, but was that the only reason? Was it the main reason?

An important clue is found in one passage where we are told that the disciples provided Jesus with a boat in which he could sit and speak and which the disciples pushed away from the shore. Why did they do this? So people couldn't press Jesus (Mark 4:1). Another way of saying it would be so people couldn't mob Jesus.

People crowded around Jesus, hoping to get close, even to touch Him. They did this hoping for blessing or, in some cases, hoping for healing. The woman with the hemorrhage shows a dramatic example of this (Mark 5:24–34). Also, in the present story, many in the crowd hoped for healing or some other tangible blessing. In fact, archaeologists and historians believe that on any given day, one-quarter of the population was ill, injured, or in some way in need of medical help.

Jesus observed Simon Peter and his friends washing their nets. He noticed, too, that they had no catch of fish. So, Jesus, the builder, suggested that Simon, the fisherman, cast out and try again. We can only imagine the look on Simon's face and the tone of his voice when he objected, "Master, we worked hard all night and caught nothing." Nevertheless, Simon—perhaps rolling his eyes—did what Jesus suggested, which resulted in an enormous catch of fish. Once again, we can only imagine the look on Simon's face—this time a very different look—and the tone of his voice, when he cried out, "Go away from me, Lord, for I am a sinful man!"

Why did Simon say this? The miraculous catch of fish revealed to Simon that Jesus was no ordinary teacher. Simon rightly sensed a miracle had taken place, that the power of God was at work in Jesus. More than that, Simon probably sensed the very presence of God in Jesus. Like other mortals in the presence of divinity, Simon became acutely aware of his sinfulness. One thinks of the prophet Isaiah when God suddenly appeared in the temple. The prophet cried out, “Woe is me, for I am ruined!” (Isaiah 6:5). So also Simon Peter. When he realizes who Jesus is, he shrinks back and confesses that he is a sinful man.

It is then that Jesus summons Simon and his companions to follow Him—to start catching people, not fish. It is then that they leave everything and become disciples of Jesus. For Simon to leave his boat and life as a fisherman is a good indicator of the awe he felt at that moment of revelation when the nets were filled with fish.

KEY TAKEAWAY

The summons to discipleship did not come out of the blue. It came in the context of dramatic revelation. The summons also came with a cost: To follow Jesus, the disciples had to leave everything. To follow Jesus today, we might not have to leave everything (and most in the early Church did not leave their property), but God does want our whole selves. It is as Paul says in one of his letters, “I do not seek what is Yours, but You” (II Corinthians 12:14).

THE STORY OF
the Disciples Who Can't Follow Jesus

Not All Who Jesus Calls Follow Him

MAIN CHARACTERS

JESUS, the principal figure in the Gospels and in the New Testament, was known as a teacher and an interpreter of Scripture. Jesus often referred to Himself as the "Son of Man," which alluded to the mysterious humanlike figure described in Daniel 7:13–14. He was also known for calling people to follow Him—some did, some didn't.

THREE WOULD-BE DISCIPLES, though initially open to following Jesus, evidently could not do so because of other commitments.

SCRIPTURE REFERENCE

As they were going along the road, someone said to Him, "I will follow You wherever You go." And Jesus said to him, "The foxes have holes and the birds of the air have nests, but the Son of Man has nowhere to lay His head." And He said to another, "Follow Me." But he said, "Lord, permit me first to go and bury my father." But He said to him, "Allow the dead to bury their own dead; but as for you, go and proclaim everywhere the kingdom of God." Another also said, "I will follow You, Lord; but first permit me to say goodbye to those at home." But Jesus said to him, "No one, after putting his hand to the plow and looking back, is fit for the kingdom of God." (Luke 9:57–62)

What You Might Assume

The men who offered to follow Jesus were not sincere. Perhaps they thought following Jesus was not difficult or brought with it no cost or would require little effort.

Jesus's retort, "Allow the dead to bury their own dead," was a bit callous and insensitive. After all, caring for one's parents is commanded in Scripture.

Refusing the man's request to say goodbye to his family was unnecessarily strict, perhaps even cruel.

Jesus was telling people to abandon their families.

What Is More Likely

The men who expressed interest in following Jesus were quite sincere. It is likely that they assumed that becoming disciples of Jesus was not much different from becoming disciples of other teachers or rabbis. Would these men be willing to sacrifice their property and security? Probably not.

Jesus's strange retort, "Allow the dead to bury their own dead," was not callous or insensitive but referred to the lengthy process of burial rituals that were common at the time.

Jesus perceived reluctance in the man who wished to say goodbye to his family. It is probable that Jesus sensed conflict. He challenged the man by alluding to Elijah's call of Elisha.

Jesus uses hyperbole to make the point that following Him costs.

The Story Behind the Scriptures

The call of Simon Peter and company is well-known. They dropped everything to follow Jesus. But what do we know of people Jesus summoned who did not drop everything and follow Him? What about people who approached Jesus and expressed interest in following Him? What happened? Why didn't they become disciples?

We usually aren't too interested in the "non-success" stories. But we should be because they can teach us a lot about the ministry of Jesus and what is involved in following Him. The first would-be follower said to Jesus, "I will follow You wherever You go." We should assume he meant it. But does he fully understand what he will be getting into? Jesus replied, "The foxes have holes and the birds of the air have nests, but the Son of Man has nowhere to lay His head." What is startling is that "the Son of Man" refers to the exalted figure in Daniel 7:13–14. The Son of Man is given the kingdom and authority. He should lay His head down on a bed in a palace. Yet, on the road in ministry, He had no place to lay His head. Ironically, animals were more comfortable! Would this would-be disciple be willing to give up the comforts of his bed and home?

The second man was willing to follow Jesus, but he needed first to bury his father. Jesus replied, "Allow the dead to bury their own dead." What on earth did Jesus mean by that? Jesus was not referring to the death and burial of the man's father but to his reburial. The Jewish people buried the dead, mourned for seven days, and then one year later gathered the bones and placed them in a niche or burial box. It is to this that the man and Jesus referred. "Lord, permit me first to go and bury my father," that is, "Permit me to re-bury my father. He died almost one year ago and soon I will gather his bones." To make the meaning clear, we may also paraphrase Jesus's reply: "Allow the dead in your family tomb to take care of what else needs to be done for your father; it is more important that you proclaim the kingdom to the living."

The third man wanted to go home and say goodbye to his family before following Jesus. Jesus replied, "No one, after putting his hand to the plow and looking back, is fit for the kingdom of God." The request to say goodbye and the reference to the plow recall Elijah's call of Elisha to be his disciple and successor (I Kings 19:19–21). When the prophet Elijah called Elisha (who was working as a plowman) to follow as his successor, Elisha was allowed to say goodbye to his family. By contrast, Jesus didn't allow it, suggesting that His call to discipleship was of much greater importance than Elijah's call of Elisha. Such a startling contrast underscores the importance of Jesus's proclamation of the kingdom of God.

KEY TAKEAWAY

Failures to follow Jesus can be just as revealing as success stories. The three would-be disciples who could not give up family and possessions to follow Jesus contrast sharply with the disciples who did give up family and possessions to follow Jesus. Their inability helps us appreciate even more the willingness of the twelve apostles to give it their all. We see in these stories that the call to discipleship should have priority over everything else. Not everyone who follows Jesus must give up home and family, but some calls to ministry do require great sacrifice. And indeed, all of us must give up our sinful ways.

THE STORY OF

Jesus Stilling the Storm

Jesus Stills the Storm

MAIN CHARACTERS

JESUS, the principal figure in the Gospels and in the New Testament, was known as a teacher who summoned disciples. He was also known as a healer, so it wasn't surprising that He attracted crowds. But, as it turns out, there was a lot more to Him.

DISCIPLES, those who followed Jesus and accompanied Him in ministry, even crowding into a small boat and crossing the Sea of Galilee.

SCRIPTURE REFERENCE

On that day, when evening came, He said to them, "Let us go over to the other side." Leaving the crowd, they took Him along with them in the boat, just as He was; and other boats were with Him. And there arose a fierce gale of wind, and the waves were breaking over the boat so much that the boat was already filling up. Jesus Himself was in the stern, asleep on the cushion; and they woke Him and said to Him, "Teacher, do You not care that we are perishing?" And He got up and rebuked the wind and said to the sea, "Hush, be still." And the wind died down and it became perfectly calm. And He said to them, "Why are you afraid? Do you still have no faith?" They became very much afraid and said to one another, "Who then is this, that even the wind and the sea obey Him?" (Mark 4:35–41)

What You Might Assume

The disciples wondered if Jesus cared about them since, after all, he was sleeping.

The disciples were overreacting. The storm wasn't that dangerous.

Jesus's calming the storm was amazing but carried no cultural or political implications.

Jesus expected too much of His disciples. They shouldn't have been afraid since He was in the boat with them.

What Is More Likely

The disciples were so terrified they said things they did not really mean and would later regret.

The disciples, especially those who had fished the Sea of Galilee for years, knew how dangerous these sudden storms could be. They knew full well that their lives were in danger, that many had drowned in these waters.

Calming a storm suggested strongly that divine power was at work in Jesus, and calming a storm implied that Jesus was greater than Caesar.

Because they had not been disciples very long, they did not fully understand who He was and the awesome power He possessed. The disciples had not yet been put to a major test of their faith. They knew Jesus had the power to heal and cast out evil spirits. But did He have power over nature itself? They were about to find out.

The Story Behind the Scriptures

To be overtaken by a storm that begins to swamp your boat is a terrifying experience. This is what happened to the disciples of Jesus, most of whom were not experienced men of the sea. Even those who were, such as Peter, Andrew, James, and John, were afraid. Indeed, they knew full well the danger. And if the men with experience were afraid, then we can hardly blame the others for being fearful.

We don't know if all twelve of Jesus's disciples were in the boat the day the storm came up. It's possible that they were. Forty years ago, a two-thousand-year-old boat submerged in mud on the Northwest Shore of the Sea of Galilee was discovered and successfully excavated. After careful cleaning and preservation, it is now on display. The boat has been studied and examined in detail. As it turns out, the boat could easily have accommodated thirteen men—six on each side and one at the stern—very much the way we imagine it in the story of the stilling of the storm.

The storm that overtook Jesus and His disciples was so violent that waves were spilling into the boat. In moments, the boat would be swamped. The disciples cried out in panic. Once awakened, Jesus commanded the water to be still. The storm ended, and the water was calm. It is no surprise that the disciples were utterly astounded. They wondered, "Who then is this, that even the wind and the sea obey Him?"

No one in the first century could hear this story and not think of claims and stories of great men who believed they possessed the power to calm storms and hush winds. One such figure was a Greek king who, in the second century BC, tried to destroy the people of Israel. "I'll make Jerusalem a Jewish cemetery," he threatened. Not long after making this threat, the king became horribly ill—so ill he couldn't walk or stand. "Thus he who had just been thinking that he could command the waves of the sea, in his superhuman arrogance, and imagining that he could weigh the high mountains in a balance, was brought down to earth and carried in a litter, making the power of God manifest to all" (II Maccabees 9:8 RSV).

Interpreters have noticed the contrast between the Greek king and

Jesus. What the king and others like him couldn't do, Jesus could. Jesus quite literally could command the wind and sea to be still. In another story, Jesus walked on water (see Mark 6:47–52), something else that Roman emperors tried to do. For example, the maniacal Emperor Caligula (ruled AD 37–41) tied hundreds of boats together, crossed over them in a chariot, and then claimed he had crossed the sea and that Poseidon, the god of the sea, feared him! What a clown! In stark contrast, Jesus made no boast; He simply spoke the word, and it happened. His disciples had never seen anything like it.

KEY TAKEAWAY

The disciples not only learned a great lesson about faith; they learned that Jesus was much more than they had assumed and imagined. It's one thing to heal and cast out evil spirits, but to command the weather? What this important story teaches is that Jesus is much more than an inspiring teacher and a kind man who helps people. He is God in the flesh, who acts with the authority of God Himself. To respond to Him in faith is to enter into a relationship with the Almighty.

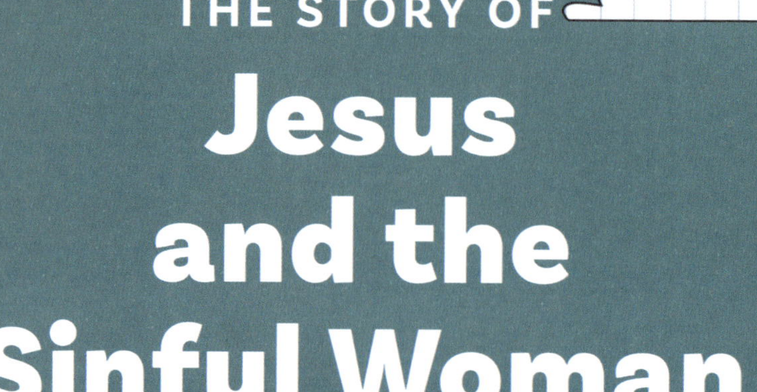

THE STORY OF

Jesus and the Sinful Woman

Jesus Assures the Woman Her Sins Are Forgiven

MAIN CHARACTERS

JESUS, the principal figure of the Gospels and the New Testament, was known for teaching and calling disciples. He often taught in synagogues and was likely invited to dinner after preaching in one.

SIMON THE PHARISEE invited Jesus to dinner in his home.

A "SINFUL" YET FORGIVEN WOMAN

JESUS'S DISCIPLES, though not mentioned, were likely all with Him.

SCRIPTURE REFERENCE.

Now one of the Pharisees was requesting Him to dine with him, and He entered the Pharisee's house and reclined at the table. And there was a woman in the city who was a sinner; and when she learned that He was reclining . . . she brought an alabaster vial of perfume, and standing behind Him at His feet, weeping, she began to wet His feet with her tears, and kept wiping them with the hair of her head, and kissing His feet and anointing them with the perfume. Now when the Pharisee who had invited Him saw this, he said to himself, "If this man were a prophet He would know . . . that she is a sinner." And Jesus answered him, "Simon, I have something to say to you." . . . "A moneylender had two debtors: one owed five hundred denarii, and the other fifty. When they were unable to repay, he graciously forgave them both. So which of them will love him more?" Simon answered . . . , "I suppose the one whom he forgave more." And He said . . . , "You have judged correctly." Turning toward the woman, He said to Simon, "Do you see this woman? I entered your house; you gave Me no water . . . but she has wet My feet with her tears . . . You gave Me no kiss; but she . . . has not ceased to kiss My feet. You did not anoint My head with oil, but she anointed My feet with perfume. For this reason I say to you, her sins, which are many, have been forgiven . . ." Then He said to her, "Your sins have been forgiven." Those . . . at the table . . . began to say . . . , "Who is this man who even forgives sins?" And He said to the woman, "Your faith has saved you; go in peace." (Luke 7:36–50)

What You Might Assume

The “sinful” woman sneaked into the Pharisee’s house, and houses in the time of Jesus are like houses today.

The woman somehow crawled under the table in order to reach Jesus’s feet.

Touching and washing Jesus’s feet was an odd, even creepy thing to do.

The woman’s sins were forgiven because she washed Jesus’s feet; it was her act of kindness that saved her.

Simon the Pharisee invited Jesus to his house in order to embarrass him.

What Is More Likely

The woman was part of the synagogue congregation, all of whom had been invited to Simon's house. But she wasn't in the house itself; like everyone else, she was in Simon's courtyard.

The woman easily accessed Jesus's feet because He was reclining, not sitting upright on a chair, and therefore, His feet were extended away from the table.

The washing of a guest's feet was a common courtesy; there was nothing creepy about it.

The woman's actions were expressions of her gratitude for forgiveness, but they were not what saved her.

Simon invited Jesus to his home for dinner out of obligation, perhaps also out of curiosity.

The Story Behind the Scriptures

The story of the sinful woman who anoints Jesus's feet raises many questions—chief among them, why Simon the Pharisee, who neglected common courtesies, invited Jesus in the first place. If the man held such a dismissive opinion of Jesus, why did he invite Him to dinner? We might also wonder how it is that a woman regarded as sinful gained access to a dinner hosted by a Pharisee. Why wasn't she stopped at the door? And what was behind Simon's thinking, "If this man were a prophet . . ."? Clearly, Simon assumed some things with which Jesus was out of step. In short, what is going on?

To fully appreciate this story, it helps to understand how people in first-century Galilee lived—and what they assumed about sinners and prophets. We might begin with how they dined. Jewish people did not sit at dinner tables in the way we might think of today. It was customary to recline rather than to sit at a table. People would lean on their left side, propping themselves up on cushions, with their feet stretched out behind them. They would sit on three sides of the low table, leaving an open side to allow for servants to easily place food on the table. Because people reclined with heads and arms close to the table and their legs away from the table, a servant could easily access their feet. It was also the custom of the day to show respect for guests by having servants wash their feet. We should assume that Simon invited Jesus to his home, along with most of the village, because Jesus had spoken in the synagogue. Simon invited Jesus out of obligation, not out of respect.

What about assumptions about prophets and sinners? It was widely assumed that as a holy man, a prophet would not touch or allow himself to be touched by anything impure or unholy. It was also assumed that a true prophet possessed clairvoyant power and so knew things about people he had never met. Because Jesus allowed a woman regarded in the village as "sinful" to touch him, Simon the Pharisee assumed Jesus did not possess clairvoyant power and, therefore, did not know what kind of woman she was. And if Jesus did not possess such power, then clearly he wasn't a true prophet—or so Simon assumed.

As it turned out, Jesus not only knew that the woman had committed many sins, but He also knew what Simon was thinking! What Simon didn't know was that the woman was responding to God's grace, which she had encountered through Jesus's preaching. By washing His feet, she was expressing her love and thankfulness. Her actions did not save her; her actions reflected her joy and gratitude for being saved. When Jesus identified the woman as a (forgiven) sinner and responded to Simon's inner thoughts, Simon then knew that Jesus possessed clairvoyant power and was indeed a prophet. Furthermore, Simon and his guests also learned that Jesus possessed the authority to forgive sinners.

KEY TAKEAWAY

The story of the sinful woman is one of the most touching stories in the Bible and highlights the boldness of Jesus's ministry to women. Having been forgiven much, the sinful woman was bursting with gratitude, so much so that she risked rejection by approaching Jesus to show that gratitude in a very risky context. In the woman's tears and in Jesus's words, we observe a moving moment of grace and forgiveness. No soul is lost, no matter how mired in sin, if that soul responds to the grace of God extended to us in His Son Jesus.

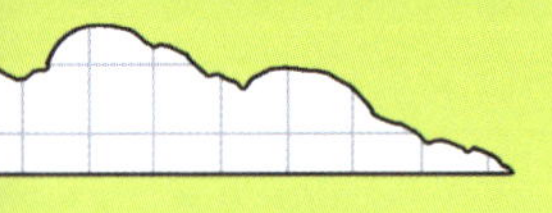

THE STORY OF

Jesus Healing the Demoniac Called Legion

Jesus Defeats a Legion of Evil Spirits

MAIN CHARACTERS

JESUS is again the central figure, displaying His power over the demonic realm in the story of the possessed man on the east side of the Sea of Galilee.

THE DISCIPLES were present with their Master but remained passive observers.

THE DEMONIAC played a major role, speaking and acting more than Jesus. Though terrifying, he surrendered and pleaded for mercy in Jesus's presence.

THE FRIGHTENED SWINEHERDERS AND CITIZENS, mostly Gentiles, were key witnesses. They had never seen such power—especially from a Jewish stranger who suddenly tamed the man who had long terrorized the region.

SCRIPTURE REFERENCE

They came to the other side of the sea, into the country of the Gerasenes. When He [Jesus] got out of the boat, immediately a man from the tombs with an unclean spirit met Him . . . and no one was able to bind him anymore, even with a chain; because he had often been bound with shackles and chains, and the chains had been torn apart . . . and no one was strong enough to subdue him. Constantly, night and day, he was screaming among the tombs and in the mountains, and gashing himself with stones. Seeing Jesus from a distance, he ran up and bowed down before Him; and shouting . . . he said, "What business do we have with each other, Jesus, Son of the Most High God? I implore You . . . do not torment me!" For He had been saying . . ., "Come out of the man, you unclean spirit!" And He was asking him, "What is your name?" And he said to Him, "My name is Legion; for we are many." And he began to implore Him . . . not to send them out of the country. Now there was a large herd of swine feeding nearby . . . The demons implored Him, saying, "Send us into the swine . . ." Jesus gave them permission. And coming out, the unclean spirits entered the swine; and the herd rushed down the steep bank into the sea . . . and they were drowned. (Mark 5:1–13)

What You Might Assume

The demonized man lived in the vicinity of Gerasa, some thirty miles southeast of the Eastern Shore of the Sea of Galilee.

The demonized man was insane, not necessarily possessed by evil spirits. After all, we cannot be sure that demons are real.

The destruction of the herd of swine was cruel.

Given the distance of Gerasa from the lake, the swine were too far away to rush headlong into the Sea of Galilee.

Jesus tricked the demons.

What Is More Likely

The demonized man lived on the cliffs overlooking the lake, and the nearby city was Gergesa, not Gerasa (or Gadara). An early and very important Church father named Origen explained that some of the scribes who made copies of the New Testament Gospels confused the obscure village of Gergesa, which was situated on the Eastern Shore of the Sea of Galilee, with the similar-sounding names Gerasa and Gadara—two much better-known cities. Origen is correct.

The demonized man was indeed possessed by evil spirits. He may also have had mental problems, but that does not rule out actual demonic possession.

The destruction of the swine was not Jesus's intention but the result of the violent and destructive nature of the demonic host.

Because Gergesa was close to the east shore of the Sea of Galilee, a stampede of swine into the lake was entirely possible.

There is no reason to think that Jesus tricked the demons.

The Story Behind the Scriptures

Most interpreters regard the story of the demonized man and the herd of pigs that drowned in the Sea of Galilee as quite possibly the strangest story in all of Scripture. It is also one of the most impressive stories in the Gospels. People in the time of Jesus feared evil spirits—not because the whole idea is creepy, but because evil spirits harmed people (see Mark 9:21-22, where a desperate father tells Jesus that an evil spirit is trying to kill his son). The demonic horde that possessed the demonized man on the Eastern Shore of the Sea of Galilee would have been especially frightful, for no one could bind him—not even with chains. His ability to break the chains and tear apart the shackles would have brought to mind the mighty Samson, whom no one could bind (Judges 16:6-12).

But the possessed man was even scarier. When asked his name, he told Jesus, "My name is Legion; for we are many" (verse 9). Hearing this, everyone in the first century would immediately think of the powerful military forces of ancient Rome, which were known as the Roman legions. These legions were well-trained, disciplined, and highly organized, making them a central part of the Roman Empire's success in expanding and maintaining its dominance. Not only that, but the nearby herd of pigs would also remind people in the time of Jesus—and in the lands of Galilee and Syria—that the Tenth Roman Legion (a highly esteemed military unit that played key roles in some of the most crucial events of the Roman Republic and Empire), whose mascot was the wild boar, was stationed nearby.

Thus, Jesus faced the greatest danger He could face: a whole legion of evil spirits whose power was so great that not even chains could restrain their pitiful human host. Already in His public ministry, demons had fallen to the ground before Jesus, begging for mercy (Mark 1; 3). But what about a whole legion?

As it turns out, "Legion" was no match for Jesus. The demonized man ran to Jesus and bowed before Him, begging not to be tormented.

The legion had surrendered and was asking for terms! Jesus accepted the surrender of the man but not that of the evil spirits. For them, there would be no mercy. Jesus sent them into the pigs (which, remember, are unclean to the Jewish people), and the herd rushed into the Sea of Galilee and drowned. Jesus saved the man and destroyed the demonic legion. When the nearby villagers arrived to see what had happened, they found the man in his right mind sitting at the feet of Jesus. They had never seen anything like it.

KEY TAKEAWAY

The great lesson of Jesus's encounter with the demonized man who called himself "Legion" is that the grace and restorative power of Jesus are unmatched and unlimited. If Jesus can heal and restore a man like that, He can heal and restore anyone. No one is beyond the reach of God's mercy and grace. Furthermore, Jesus showed that He not only has control and dominion over the weather and over things on earth, but He also has dominion and power over the spiritual whelm.

THE STORY OF

Jesus and the Woman with a Hemorrhage

Jesus Assures the Woman Her Faith Has Made Her Well

MAIN CHARACTERS

JESUS once again is leading His disciples, teaching and healing as He encounters people.

A WOMAN with a hemorrhage, whom doctors could not heal.

THE DISCIPLES accompanied Jesus, but in this story, they played the role of observers.

CROWDS witnessed Jesus's extraordinary power at work.

SCRIPTURE REFERENCE

. . . and a large crowd was following Him and pressing in on Him. A woman who had had a hemorrhage for twelve years, and had endured much at the hands of many physicians, and had spent all that she had and was not helped at all, but rather had grown worse —after hearing about Jesus, she came up in the crowd behind Him and touched His cloak. For she thought, "If I just touch His garments, I will get well." Immediately the flow of her blood was dried up; and she felt in her body that she was healed of her affliction. Immediately Jesus, perceiving in Himself that the power proceeding from Him had gone forth, turned around in the crowd and said, "Who touched My garments?" And His disciples said to Him, "You see the crowd pressing in on You, and You say, 'Who touched Me?'" And He looked around to see the woman who had done this. But the woman fearing and trembling, aware of what had happened to her, came and fell down before Him and told Him the whole truth. And He said to her, "Daughter, your faith has made you well; go in peace and be healed of your affliction." (Mark 5:24–34)

What You Might Assume

All physicians in antiquity were incompetent, and the evangelist Mark intended to denigrate them in this story. We may get this impression because in his version of the story, the evangelist Luke, who was himself a physician (see Col 4:14 "Luke, the beloved physician"), omitted many of Mark's details about how the doctors failed the woman.

The woman with the hemorrhage was in a state of impurity, and touching Jesus was presumptuous and perhaps even a violation of Jewish law.

Everyone can be healed.

For some strange reason, Jesus did not know who had touched Him.

What Is More Likely

Though physicians often did not enjoy good reputations, some were caring and to some degree were competent. There is some ancient testimony to the effect that some doctors truly helped, even healed, their patients. Also, not all doctors were greedy cheats, as sometimes was claimed in our ancient sources.

The woman may not have been in a state of impurity, and therefore, touching Jesus was not in itself necessarily inappropriate. The main point is that she was truly ill, and no one could cure her.

Faith plays an important role in healing; not all are healed because not all have faith in Jesus. Also, God has a sovereign plan and purpose that goes beyond individual circumstances. Healing may not always be in God's will for a person at a particular time.

Jesus knew who had touched Him and why, but He wanted to engage the woman and assure her that she was indeed healed and that her faith had played a very important role.

The Story Behind the Scriptures

Imagine the daring, the desperation, the faith that led the woman with the hemorrhage to weave her way close enough to Jesus to reach out surreptitiously and touch the edge of His garment. It is widely assumed that she should not have touched Jesus because she was in a state of impurity. In Jesus's day, religiously observant Jews were very concerned with purity: Pots and pans had to be washed properly, hands had to be washed a certain way, people were expected to immerse themselves, and so forth (see Mark 7:3–4). But whether or not the woman in our story was ritually impure, it is not likely that merely touching Jesus would have been viewed as conveying impurity to Him. It is more likely that her action would have been viewed as presumptuous—a woman touching a man who was not her husband. But we suspect her real reason for sneaking up behind Jesus, to touch Him without anyone noticing, was to protect her privacy. If she had asked Jesus for healing, He might have asked her what was wrong. And she didn't want to say. Indeed, if her need became public, she might be severely chastised.

Her desperation is seen not only in her coming up behind Jesus and touching Him, but also in interrupting what was going on. She surely knew, along with the whole crowd, that Jesus was accompanying a desperate father to his home to treat his daughter, who was near death.

The evangelist Mark tells us that the woman with the hemorrhage had spent all her money on doctors, and none of them had helped her. Indeed, her condition had only worsened.

Ancient readers would have readily identified with this woman's plight. First-century Roman geographer Pliny cynically remarked that the Greek doctors "have conspired together to murder all foreigners with their physic," which "they do for a fee!" He, of course, has exaggerated, but the Roman world was filled with quacks and fake doctors. Pliny also tells us that he has seen gravestones with inscriptions that read, "It was a crowd of physicians that killed me." Historians remind us of the bitter words of the dying Emperor Hadrian (ruled AD 117–138): "Many physicians have slain a king!" If emperors couldn't get competent medical care, who could? Not only was medical care dubious, it was expensive. A woman in

Egypt wrote to her sister complaining that seeing doctors "wasted a lot of money." And many more examples could be cited.

Accordingly, the evangelist Mark's comment that the poor woman "had endured much at the hands of many physicians" and "had spent all that she had and was not helped at all, but rather had grown worse" would have struck a sympathetic chord with most who heard this story. But when she touched Jesus, believing that He could help her, she was instantly healed. When the woman kneeled before Jesus, she must have been filled with awe and gratitude. Jesus assured her, "Daughter, your faith has made you well." Addressing her as "daughter" was a term of endearment. To her surprise, Jesus not only assured the woman that she had been healed, but He lovingly instructed her to "go in peace," which in Hebrew implies wholeness, thus restoring her place in society, as well as her health. Her encounter with Jesus would never be forgotten.

KEY TAKEAWAY

On the surface, this intriguing story again shows Jesus's power to heal an incurable illness; however, the key point here is that faith in Jesus opens doors to the power of God and brings about healing, restoration, and a merciful touch by God. While it does not tell us that we will always be healed, it shows us what it looks like to reach out in faith to Jesus, in times of pain and heartache. It shows us how to put our faith into action: Reach out, step up, touch, and do what's needed, even if we feel fear and trepidation. Jesus's powerful work and loving response invite us to trust Him. He is sufficient to meet whatever need we have.

THE STORY OF

Jesus Restoring Life to a Man's Daughter

Jesus Raises Up the Daughter of Jairus, the Leader of the Synagogue

MAIN CHARACTERS:

JESUS once again is leading His disciples, teaching and healing as He encounters people.

JAIRUS, a synagogue official—or ruler—was likely a prominent man in the town of Capernaum, where Jesus often stayed.

THE DAUGHTER of Jairus is gravely ill, prompting her father to seek out Jesus for help.

THE DISCIPLES, who accompanied Jesus, witness His teachings and miracles firsthand.

FAMILY, FRIENDS, AND RELATIVES of Jairus and his daughter mourn when the girl died, and some of them laugh when Jesus says the girl "has not died."

SCRIPTURE REFERENCE

One of the synagogue officials named Jairus came up, and on seeing Him (Jesus), fell at His feet and implored Him earnestly, saying, "My little daughter is at the point of death; please come and lay Your hands on her, so that she will get well and live." And He went off with him . . . . they came from the house of the synagogue official, saying, "Your daughter has died; why trouble the Teacher anymore?" But Jesus, overhearing what was being spoken, said to the synagogue official, "Do not be afraid any longer, only believe." And He allowed no one to accompany Him, except Peter and James and John the brother of James. They came to the house of the synagogue official; and He saw a commotion, and people loudly weeping and wailing. And entering in, He said to them, "Why make a commotion and weep? The child has not died, but is asleep." They began laughing at Him. But putting them all out, He took along the child's father and mother and His own companions, and entered the room where the child was. Taking the child by the hand, He said to her, "Talitha kum!" (which translated means, "Little girl, I say to you, get up!"). Immediately the girl got up and began to walk, for she was twelve years old. And immediately they were completely astounded. (Mark 5:22–24, 35–42)

What You Might Assume

If Jesus had prioritized things differently, the little girl might not have died. The woman's condition did not require immediate attention, but the little girl's condition did.

The little girl was only asleep; she really hadn't died.

Jesus's words "Talitha kum" are mysterious, perhaps even magical.

It was no big deal to touch the deceased child.

What Is More Likely

!

Jesus knew what He was doing and that God's will would be done.

The little girl really was dead; those attending her were not mistaken.

The words "Talitha kum" are ordinary Aramaic words; there was nothing magical or mysterious about them.

It was a big deal, for touching the dead made one impure. But Jesus possessed the power to make the impure pure and, as we shall see, to make the dead alive.

The Story Behind the Scriptures

In the days of Jesus, life was short and often painful. Human longevity ranged only into the twenties and thirties. Most of you who are reading these words would have died long ago if health care today was anything like it was two thousand years ago. It is no wonder that crowds followed Jesus, sometimes interfering with His attempts to teach. The study of inscriptions, skeletal remains, and documents that survived from antiquity leads to the conclusion that only one-half of children reached adulthood. Women often died in childbirth. Young children often succumbed to illnesses that today are easily prevented and cured.

The tragedy of early death is abundantly attested in the epitaphs left behind by grieving parents. One epitaph reads: "Hilarion, daughter of Philip, untimely dead, friend of all, who caused pain to none, excellent girl, farewell. About 6 years old." Another reads: "Philoution, excellent girl, farewell, friend of all, untimely dead. About 15 years old." And in this last one, we read that young Junia Procula "left her wretched father and mother in grief." The story of Jairus and his daughter could have ended the same way had it not been for the appearance of Jesus.

We can easily imagine an anxious father hurrying Jesus along the road to his house, only to be interrupted by the woman suffering from a hemorrhage. Jesus healed the woman and spoke words of assurance; all the while, Jairus must have been going out of his mind with worry and impatience.

Finally, Jesus turned toward Jairus's house, only to be met by a relative with the tragic news that his little girl had died. No need to trouble the Teacher further. We can only imagine the anguish Jairus felt. If only he had found Jesus sooner! If only they had *run* to the house! Perhaps the girl could have been saved. But Jesus told the man, "Do not be afraid any longer, only believe." Believe *what*? The girl had died!

When Jesus entered the house to find the young girl laid out on a couch, perhaps already being prepared for burial, He startled everyone by stating, "The child has not died, but is asleep." Family and friends laughed; they knew death when they saw it. The little girl was most certainly dead. But Jesus spoke of death as little more than sleep because the power at work in Him is such that reviving the dead is like waking a sleeping person.

Jesus took the girl by the hand—thus ignoring concerns about corpse impurity (which in the minds of some required ritual bathing and even a time of self-quarantine)—and spoke the Aramaic words, *Talitha, kum*, which means, "Little girl, get up." These are not magical words; they are the everyday words of Aramaic-speaking Jews who live in Galilee. The little girl heard, awakened, got up, and walked. Everyone was astounded. They had never seen anything like it.

KEY TAKEAWAY

The power of Jesus is seen again and again. He not only heals what no ordinary doctor can heal, but He can even raise up the dead and renew life. The ultimate gift that Jesus offers to all is life in the world to come. He cares deeply for all of us, and while we at times have to wait or feel that He is not paying close attention, He will ignore no one.

THE STORY OF Jesus Multiplying the Loaves and Fish

Jesus Multiplies Loaves and Fish for a Hungry Crowd

MAIN CHARACTERS

JESUS has been teaching crowds of people all day, with no break even for a meal.

THE DISCIPLES accompanied Jesus, and when needed, they assisted in distributing the loaves and fish.

A LARGE CROWD of people was listening to Jesus teach. We should assume, too, that some were ill and hoping for healing.

SCRIPTURE REFERENCE

When it was already quite late, His disciples came to Him and said, "This place is desolate and it is already quite late; send them away so that they may go into the surrounding countryside and villages and buy themselves something to eat." But He answered them, "You give them something to eat!" And they said to Him, "Shall we go and spend two hundred denarii on bread and give them something to eat?" And He said to them, "How many loaves do you have? Go look!" And when they found out, they said, "Five, and two fish." And He commanded them all to sit down by groups on the green grass. They sat down in groups of hundreds and of fifties. And He took the five loaves and the two fish, and looking up toward heaven, He blessed the food and broke the loaves and He kept giving them to the disciples to set before them; and He divided up the two fish among them all. They all ate and were satisfied, and they picked up twelve full baskets of the broken pieces, and also of the fish. There were five thousand men who ate the loaves. (Mark 6:35–44)

What You Might Assume

The “desolate place” is a desert or perhaps a great distance from the nearest village.

The people are simply hungry and perhaps tired.

Jesus was expecting too much from His disciples.

There were only five thousand who were fed.

What Is More Likely

Jesus and the crowd were far away from a village where they could find food. They were not in a desert but in an area that was sparsely inhabited.

Many of the people were not only hungry and tired but also unwell. Many were probably malnourished and, in their weakened state, in no condition to return home.

Jesus was setting up another learning situation for the disciples, as well as the crowd.

There were five thousand men, *plus* women and children.

The Story Behind the Scriptures

Jesus had performed some amazing miracles, but multiplying five loaves and two fish so that more than five thousand people could eat their fill (with food left over!) was beyond all expectations. And, in a world of hungry and malnourished people, a miracle like this would have been especially appreciated. But there's a lot more to this miracle than meets the eye.

The miraculous feeding of the multitude would have immediately reminded the Jewish people of two famous historical figures in biblical history. The first and most obvious was Moses, through whom God provided the wandering Israelites with bread (i.e., manna) in the wilderness for forty years. This gave rise to the belief that when the Messiah should appear, bread would once again be made available in abundance. Hunger would be a thing of the past.

The other figure this miracle would have brought to mind was the great prophet Elisha, who ministered in Israel long ago. Back in the days of Elisha, there was a terrible famine. On top of that, the prophets of God had to keep a low profile, for Israel's pagan queen was out to kill them. For this reason, they kept to themselves in an out-of-the-way place. They had no food, and they were hungry. Then, someone brought a bag of food containing twenty loaves and ears of grain. Elisha commanded:

"Give them to the people that they may eat." His attendant said, "What, will I set this before a hundred men?" But he said, "Give them to the people that they may eat, for thus says the Lord, 'They shall eat and have some left over.'" So he set it before them, and they ate and had some left over, according to the word of the Lord. (II Kings 4:42–44)

The story of the feeding of the one hundred is very similar to the feeding of the five thousand. Not only did everyone have enough to eat, there was food "left over." There are some obvious differences too: Elisha fed one hundred with twenty loaves and a few ears of corn; Jesus fed five thousand with five loaves and two fish!

So, what is so important about miraculous feedings? Well, long ago, the prophet Isaiah foretold that in the last days, God would provide His hungry people with abundant food: "The Lord of hosts will prepare a lavish banquet for all peoples on this mountain . . ." (Isaiah 25:6). Jewish interpreters believed this prophecy would be fulfilled when the last made His appearance and the kingdom of God had at least come in power. The Jewish men of Qumran, famous for their Dead Sea Scrolls, believed that the Messiah would come and all the great men of Israel would sit next to him at the banqueting table. Jesus makes use of this image in one of His parables (Luke 14:15–24). He teaches that the poor and sick would sit at this banquet table in the very seats of honor!

What made the miracle of the loaves so important wasn't simply that hungry people were fed; it was proof that Jesus was the Messiah and that through His ministry, the kingdom of God someday would appear.

KEY TAKEAWAY

The story of the feeding miracle is astonishing; it underscores God's willingness and ability to provide both spiritually and physically for His people through the ministry of His Son Jesus. But it also assures us that the promised kingdom of God will arrive and that Jesus, who proclaimed the coming kingdom of God, knew what He was talking about and had the authority to promise it. A big takeaway for us is knowing that the kingdom of God is not just talk but is power and reality (I Corinthians 2:4–5).

THE STORY OF

Jesus Rebuking His Angry Disciples

Jesus Rebukes His Disciples

MAIN CHARACTERS

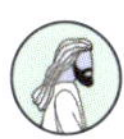

JESUS is the principal figure in our story. He is leading his men south, from Galilee to Jerusalem, which is situated in Judea. He has decided to take a direct route, which means passing through Samaria, a region that lies between Galilee to the north and Judea to the south.

THE DISCIPLES of Jesus accompany their Master; they are fully aware of the hard feelings between Jews and Samaritans. We should imagine that they are on the lookout for any hostility or insult.

SAMARITANS in our story say nothing, but they do something that in the culture of the day would been considered very offensive: They offer no hospitality to Jesus. In effect, they shoo Jesus away.

SCRIPTURE REFERENCE

When the days were approaching for His ascension, He was determined to go to Jerusalem; and He sent messengers on ahead of Him, and they went and entered a village of the Samaritans to make arrangements for Him. But they did not receive Him, because He was traveling toward Jerusalem. When His disciples James and John saw this, they said, "Lord, do You want us to command fire to come down from heaven and consume them?" But He turned and rebuked them, [and said, "You do not know what kind of spirit you are of; for the Son of Man did not come to destroy men's lives, but to save them."] And they went on to another village. (Luke 9:51–56)

What You Might Assume

Samaritans were entirely at fault for this unfriendly exchange.

Samaritans held theological views that were considered incomplete or even heretical.

The disciples' desire to call fire down from heaven was random and extreme.

What Is More Likely

!

Jewish animosity toward the Samaritan people was as much the fault of the Jewish people as it was the fault of the Samaritans. They have a long shared history—and they're family; they need to reconnect.

The Samaritans hold similar views and, indeed, regard the Law of Moses as sacred, authoritative Scripture.

The disciples' desire to call fire down from heaven was based on the example of Elijah in Scripture. Their impulse may have been extreme, but it wasn't crazy.

The Story Behind the Scriptures

The disciples of Jesus once asked if they could call down fire from heaven to destroy a Samaritan village that refused to welcome Him—a shocking request, considering Jesus's message. To understand why they would suggest such a thing, it's important to consider two key events in biblical history. First is the long history—some of it recorded in Scripture—of war and hatred between Jews and Samaritans. It all began when the northern tribes of the kingdom of Israel broke away from the two southern tribes, Judah and Benjamin. From time to time, the two kingdoms fought. Sometimes, the Jewish people of the South were very much at fault. Because the northern kingdom called their capital city Samaria, the Israelites of the north became known as Samaritans.

In the days of Jesus, ill-feeling between Samaritans and Jews continued. If traveling south, Jews in Galilee would cross the Jordan to bypass Samaria and then recross the Jordan when they reached Judea.

But the craziest story involving Samaria is found in the Bible. The famous prophet, Elijah, annoyed the kings of Samaria by criticizing them for their idolatry and polytheism. The king of Samaria sent a captain and fifty soldiers to bring Elijah to the palace. The captain spoke to Elijah: "O man of God, the king says, 'Come down.'" And Elijah replied, "If I am a man of God, let fire come down from heaven and consume you and your fifty men" (II Kings 1:9–10 NKJV). And that's what happened—fire came down from heaven and consumed the captain and his fifty soldiers. The king sent another captain and fifty, and the same thing happened (II Kings 1:11–12). The king sent a third captain and his fifty, but this time, the captain dismounted, and with humility, he addressed Elijah, "O man of God, please let my life and the lives of these fifty servants of yours be precious in your sight." Elijah went with him (II Kings 1:13).

James and John, the "Sons of Thunder" (Mark 3:17), alluded to the story of Elijah when they suggested calling down fire on a Samaritan village for rejecting Jesus. They believed that, as fire once judged disrespect toward Elijah, it should now judge disrespect toward God's Son.

To their surprise, Jesus had a different view and rebuked His disciples. Some ancient manuscripts of the Greek New Testament don't tell us what Jesus said, but some manuscripts do. According to them, Jesus said: "You do not know what kind of spirit you are of; for the Son of Man did not come to destroy men's lives, but to save them" (verses 55–56). That sounds like Jesus!

But why did the Samaritan villagers refuse to receive Jesus, to show Him and His disciples at least some hospitality? The Gospel passage says they refused Jesus because "He was traveling toward Jerusalem" (verse 53), implying that His concern lay with the Jewish people and no one else. The Samaritans sensed this and so, in effect, were saying, "If Jesus has business with Jerusalem, then He has no business with us."

The disciples got it, and they were offended. But Jesus wasn't. His mission as the Son of Man was to save lives, not destroy them. Even on the cross—what offense could be greater?—Jesus said, "Father, forgive them" (Luke 23:34).

KEY TAKEAWAY

It is only human nature to react in anger when one is slighted or when we feel what we believe to be righteous indignation. Jesus knows there will be a time for God's righteous anger, but that time is not now. Jesus sets the example: Those who follow Him are to rise above the prejudices and long-held grievances. Jesus has made it clear that His mission is to save and restore all humans, and He invites us to join Him.

THE STORY OF

the Son of the Vineyard Owner

Jesus Tells the Parable of the Wicked Vineyard Tenants

MAIN CHARACTERS

JESUS AND HIS DISCIPLES are in Jerusalem, teaching in the temple precincts.

THE CROWDS AND DISCIPLES are listening to Jesus.

RULING PRIESTS, ELDERS, AND SCRIBES hear Jesus teach and don't like what they hear.

SCRIPTURE REFERENCE

A man PLANTED A VINEYARD AND PUT A WALL AROUND IT, AND DUG A VAT UNDER THE WINE PRESS AND BUILT A TOWER, and rented it out to vine-growers and went on a journey. At the harvest time he sent a slave to the vine-growers, in order to receive some of the produce of the vineyard from the vine-growers. They took him, and beat him and sent him away empty-handed. Again he sent them another slave, and they wounded him in the head, and treated him shamefully. And he sent another, and that one they killed; and so with many others, beating some and killing others. He had one more to send, a beloved son; he sent him last of all to them, saying, "They will respect my son." But those vine-growers said to one another, "This is the heir; come, let us kill him, and the inheritance will be ours!" They took him, and killed him and threw him out of the vineyard. What will the owner of the vineyard do? He will come and destroy the vine-growers, and will give the vineyard to others. (Mark 12:1–9)

What You Might Assume

The parable of the vineyard is told with no particular context in mind.

The parable of the vineyard is an allegory of Israel's history.

The Jewish people mostly thought alike.

What Is More Likely

!

The parable of the vineyard actually answers the question that has been put to Jesus, demanding to know by what authority He does what He does.

The parable of the vineyard has more to do with the religious leaders' refusal to obey God.

The Jewish people held very different views, with some wholeheartedly agreeing with Jesus and others very much in disagreement.

The Story Behind the Scriptures

Earlier in Mark (11:27–28), the ruling priests and elders demanded of Jesus, "By what authority are You doing these things, or who gave You this authority to do these things?" They asked this because they were outraged over Jesus's criticism of the temple policies and His hint that the temple might be destroyed (Mark 11:15–18). Jesus countered with a question about the source of the authority of the popular John the Baptist. Because the ruling priests wouldn't answer, Jesus also refused to answer. But a moment later, He does answer the question—though not directly. He answered their question with a parable, a parable like no other.

In the parable, the tenant farmers refuse to give what is owed to the owner. The owner sends servants, who are roughly treated. Finally, the owner sends his son. Surely, they will respect him. But, of course, they don't; they murder him! Believe it or not, we actually have written accounts from antiquity that report such things.

Given the realities and dangers of debt collecting in antiquity, why on earth would the owner of the vineyard keep sending servants? And, especially, why would he send his son? Even more crazy is the fact that the owner of the vineyard in Jesus's parable represents God himself. How could Jesus have told such a parable if it portrayed God in such a dubious light?

Actually, that is how many parables functioned in antiquity. They portrayed characters—even God—behaving in unexpected ways. Parables often indulge in wild exaggeration to make a point.

Jesus and His hearers would have been familiar with these kinds of parables. In one parable, a rabbi speaks of an incautious king who, against the advice of his friends, entrusts his kingdom, palace, and son to the care of a corrupt guardian. The king departs, and the corrupt guardian plunders the kingdom, burns down the palace, and murders the king's son. When the king returns and sees what has happened, he weeps, pulls out his hair, and says, "Woe is me! How foolish I have been, how senselessly I acted in this kingdom of mine in entrusting my son to a wicked guardian!" (*Seder Elijah Rabbah* §28, Author Translation). Incredibly, God is the incautious king! If Jewish rabbis who love and respect God could tell a parable like that, Jesus could tell a parable that makes the same point: God keeps giving people chances, even putting His own Son at risk.

Parables help hearers—ancient and modern—to appreciate the enormity of God's love for humanity and the enormity of humanity's sin. The shocking contrast illustrated in them reveals the depth of God's grace and love.

KEY TAKEAWAY

The shocker of this story is that God knew full well what would happen to Jesus, His Son, yet He sent Him anyway. God knows what every outcome will be; Jesus knows too. But out of love for humanity, Jesus leans into His mission—a mission of redemption and salvation.

The Disciples Return to Jesus to Report Their Success

MAIN CHARACTERS

 **JESUS** is again the principal figure; He has sent His disciples out to preach, heal, and cast out evil spirits.

 **THE DISCIPLES,** who have returned to Jesus, are filled with excitement, having experienced the power of the Holy Spirit in their preaching and healing.

 **RELIGIOUS AUTHORITIES,** who expressed skepticism about the source of Jesus's power to cast out evil spirits, confront Him.

SCRIPTURE REFERENCE

The seventy returned with joy, saying, "Lord, even the demons are subject to us in Your name." And He said to them, "I was watching Satan fall from heaven like lightning. "Behold, I have given you authority to tread on serpents and scorpions, and over all the power of the enemy, and nothing will injure you. Nevertheless do not rejoice in this, that the spirits are subject to you, but rejoice that your names are recorded in heaven." (Luke 10:17–20)

"But if I cast out demons by the finger of God, then the kingdom of God has come upon you." (Luke 11:20)

What You Might Assume

Demons are not real and, therefore, are not dangerous; or...

Demons are real. They can harm us, and therefore, we should fear them.

Serpents and scorpions refer to earthly snakes and scorpions.

When people in Jesus's day attributed mental or physical illness to demon possession, they were probably just being superstitious.

What Is More Likely

Demons are indeed real, and they are dangerous.

Demons cannot harm those who follow Jesus.

Serpents and scorpions actually refer to demonic spirits.

People in Jesus's day, as well as today, can be demon-possessed.

The Story Behind the Scriptures

In the time of Jesus, everyone—Jews and Gentiles alike—feared demons. Unclean spirits haunted cemeteries, dumps, and places regarded as unclean. They desired to haunt and, if possible, to inhabit humans. They caused physical illness and insanity. They attacked humans, trying to injure and kill, and they attacked all ages. In view of these fears, we shouldn't be surprised that there were physicians and professional exorcists. Jewish exorcists had some success, thanks in part to their piety, prayers, and faith in the God of Abraham. Some exorcists invoked the name of Jesus—even though they were not part of Jesus's following—and apparently did so with some success (see Mark 9:38–40, though not always: see Acts 19:13–17).

It was widely believed that Satan, who opposed God's work and sought to corrupt humanity, functioned more or less as the commander of the demons. Whether all demons obeyed Satan is unknown, but that the Evil One influenced them is likely.

In the Old Testament, it is believed that the Serpent that tempted Eve and caused the moral and spiritual fall of Adam and Eve (see Genesis 3) was none other than Satan. Ancient interpreters believed that the prophet Isaiah spoke of Satan himself, who wished to reign in heaven, even to take God's place (Isaiah 14:12-14).

It is in this context that we should understand Jesus's startling declaration when the disciples returned from their mission, telling Jesus, "[E]ven the demons are subject to us in Your name." Jesus replied, "I was watching Satan fall from heaven like lightning." Jesus seemed to be saying that the prophecy of Isaiah had been fulfilled: Satan was cast out of heaven; the end of his malevolent career was at hand. Jesus said Satan's fall was "like lightning," which in the minds of His contemporaries signified regime change: The rule of Satan was collapsing before the advancing rule of God!

Jesus further astounded His disciples by telling them, "I have given you authority to tread on serpents and scorpions." This statement recalls the divine promise in Genesis 3, where God says to the serpent, "He shall bruise you on the head" (verse 15). Ancient interpreters understood this verse as prophesying that the Messiah would crush the head of Satan and his evil allies. Jesus's words, "tread on serpents and scorpions" (understood as demonic spirits), imply that the prophecy of Genesis was also being fulfilled in His ministry.

Jesus also assured His disciples (and this assurance applies to us too) that "nothing will injure" them; that is, Satan and his evil allies cannot harm the followers of Jesus. This is good to know, but the really good news is that our "names are recorded in heaven."

Trying to undermine the significance of His ministry, critics of Jesus called into question the importance of the exorcisms. In response, Jesus declared: "[I]f I cast out demons by the finger of God, then the kingdom of God has come upon you." Logic alone supports what Jesus has said, but His curious expression, "the finger of God," recalls what Pharaoh's magicians had to admit long ago: The power at work in Moses and Aaron was not the result of magic and trickery; it was "the finger of God" (Exodus 8:19), that is, it was the very work of God. So it is with regard to Jesus's power over Satan and his evil allies: The power of God is at work.

KEY TAKEAWAY

The author of I John assures his readers, "[G]reater is He who is in you than he who is in the world" (I John 4:4); that is, the Spirit of Jesus Christ, which resides in His followers is greater than Satan who resides in the world. The author of I John can say this because he witnessed firsthand that power at work in the ministry of Jesus. This great truth gives us confidence and peace. Not only are we protected here on earth, but our names are recorded in heaven—a guarantee of salvation—for all eternity.

THE STORY OF

the Parable of the Good Samaritan

Jesus Teaches the Scholar About His Neighbors

MAIN CHARACTERS

JESUS is traveling south toward Jerusalem and teaching along the way.

A SCRIPTURE SCHOLAR approaches Jesus to ask Him about the most important commandment in the Law of Moses.

PRIESTS AND LEVITES, as religious authorities, are presumed to know how to fulfill the Law of Moses.

A SAMARITAN, despised by Jews, is viewed with suspicion because it is assumed that Samaritans do not properly keep the Law of Moses.

SCRIPTURE REFERENCE

Jesus replied and said, "A man was going down from Jerusalem to Jericho, and fell among robbers, and they stripped him and beat him, and went away leaving him half dead. And by chance a priest was going down on that road, and when he saw him, he passed by on the other side. Likewise a Levite also ... passed by on the other side. But a Samaritan, who was on a journey, came upon him; and when he saw him, he felt compassion, and came to him and bandaged up his wounds, pouring oil and wine on them; and he put him on his own beast, and brought him to an inn . . . On the next day he took out two denarii and gave them to the innkeeper and said, 'Take care of him . . . when I return I will repay you.' Which of these three do you think proved to be a neighbor to the man . . .?" And he said, "The one who showed mercy toward him." Then Jesus said to him, "Go and do the same." (Luke 10:30–37)

What You Might Assume

The Scripture scholar to whom Jesus spoke the parable did not question Jesus sincerely.

The priest and Levite, who did not help the injured man, were callous and indifferent to human needs.

The parable of the good Samaritan is an allegory about Jesus and God's redemptive plan.

The Scripture scholar was unhappy with Jesus's teaching.

Neighbors are those who live nearby.

What Is More Likely

The Scripture scholar was very sincere, respected Jesus, and wanted to know His opinion.

The priest and Levite did not help the injured man because they thought he was dead and wanted to avoid the risk of being assaulted or becoming ritually impure.

The parable is not an allegory but an illustration that answers the question, "Who is my neighbor?"

The Scripture scholar was fully persuaded by Jesus and abandoned his prejudice against Samaritans.

Scripture understands "neighbors" as those near us on any occasion.

The Story Behind the Scriptures

The Jews of Galilee to the north and Jerusalem and Judea to the south disliked their Samaritan neighbors who lived between Galilee and Judea. Jews were convinced that Samaritans really weren't Israelites (at best, they were only half-breeds) and did not keep the Law of Moses properly. Some Jews said some really nasty things about Samaritans (and, alas, Samaritans returned the favor). On top of that, violent incidents also took place, pitting Jews against Samaritans, which only made matters worse. Nevertheless, Jews and Samaritans were neighbors, and that fact comes into play in the exchange between the Jewish scholar of Scripture and Jesus.

One day, a scholar—which has an original literal meaning of "lawyer," or expert in the Law of Moses—asked Jesus what he must do to inherit eternal life (Luke 10:25-29). Jesus asked him what the Law says and how he understands it. The scholar answered well: to love God with all one is and all one has (Deuteronomy 6:5) and to love one's neighbor (Leviticus 19:18). Jesus assured him that he answered correctly. But, the scholar still had reservations. Who was his neighbor? In Hebrew and Greek, as well as in our modern English, neighbor is literally "near one," that is, one who is nearby. That is what worried the scholar. Was he required to love all who were near him?

Jesus answered the scholar's question by telling the famous parable of the good Samaritan (Luke 10:30-35). Jesus taught that a "neighbor" is anyone near you—someone you can reach out to and help. In the parable, a man was traveling from Jerusalem to Jericho. He was likely a Jewish man, since both cities were predominantly Jewish. Along the way, he was attacked by robbers, beaten, and left for dead. Three men came near him, so in effect, three strangers became the man's neighbors. The two who knew the Law of Moses best—the priest and the Levite—did not stop to help the injured man. The third man—the Samaritan—did stop and help and so demonstrated love for one's neighbor, as the Law of Moses commands.

The scholar acknowledged the point Jesus has made. How could he not? After all, in the Old Testament Scripture, we find the story of other good Samaritans, who bandaged, clothed, and returned to Jericho several wounded men from Judah—after fighting them in battle! (See II Chronicles 28:8–15).

The scholar replied to Jesus, "The one who showed mercy toward him." By using the word "mercy," he alluded to Deuteronomy 7:2, 16 (show no favor, pity, or mercy to idolaters in the land of Israel), a passage that was sometimes unfairly applied to Samaritans. The scholar has admitted that contrary to very prejudicial assumptions, the Samaritan showed mercy to a Jewish man—despite the fact that Jews were encouraged to show no mercy to Samaritans. In doing so, the Samaritan proved love for his neighbor and fulfilled the Law of Moses.

KEY TAKEAWAY

Loving people we don't know or don't like is very hard. Yet, the Law of Moses commands us to do just that; so does Jesus. Imagine a world in which all of us obeyed that command. Hatred, strife, war—all of it—would vanish overnight. What Jesus has affirmed and what the inquiring scholar has accepted has the potential to transform the world. Let it first transform us, and then let's go from there.

THE STORY OF

Martha and Mary at Home with Jesus

Martha Complains to Jesus About Mary's Not Helping

MAIN CHARACTERS

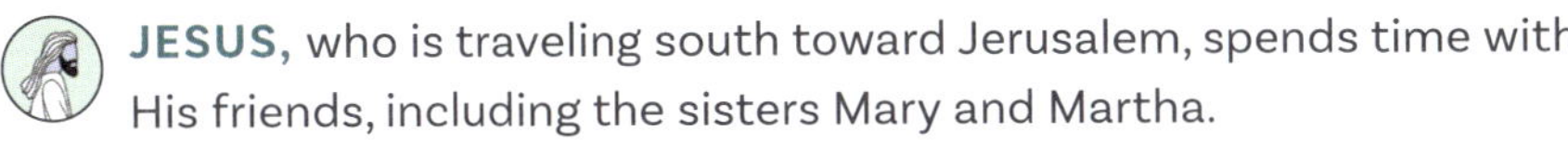

JESUS, who is traveling south toward Jerusalem, spends time with His friends, including the sisters Mary and Martha.

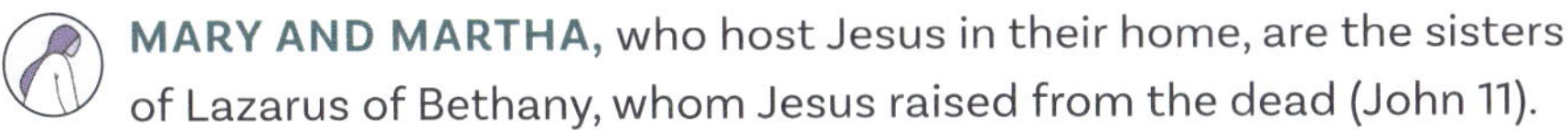

MARY AND MARTHA, who host Jesus in their home, are the sisters of Lazarus of Bethany, whom Jesus raised from the dead (John 11).

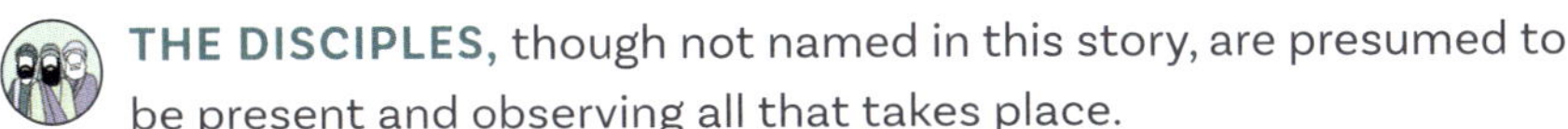

THE DISCIPLES, though not named in this story, are presumed to be present and observing all that takes place.

SCRIPTURE REFERENCE

Now as they were traveling along, He entered a village; and a woman named Martha welcomed Him into her home. She had a sister called Mary, who was seated at the Lord's feet, listening to His word. But Martha was distracted with all her preparations; and she came up to Him and said, "Lord, do You not care that my sister has left me to do all the serving alone? Then tell her to help me." But the Lord answered and said to her, "Martha, Martha, you are worried and bothered about so many things; but only one thing is necessary, for Mary has chosen the good part, which shall not be taken away from her." (Luke 10:38–42)

What You Might Assume

Mary is shirking her responsibility.

There is nothing unusual in a woman being taught.

Martha's complaint is petty.

Jesus is oblivious to Martha's concerns.

What Is More Likely

Mary has sensed how special the moment is.

Jesus is not opposed to women being taught.

Though Martha's complaint is understandable, she has missed the uniqueness and potential of the moment.

Jesus fully understood Martha's complaint but wanted to point out to her Mary's recognition of what is truly important.

The Story Behind the Scriptures

In the Gospel of Luke, we often encounter Jesus dining with disciples, friends, and even critics. We think of Jesus enjoying a great feast with Levi, eating a meal with Simon the Pharisee, eating yet more meals with Pharisees, and sometimes with sinners and tax collectors. Plus, several of Jesus's parables feature banquets. Most of these events and parables are found only in Luke.

Interpreters suspect the frequency of dinner settings in Luke is intended to emphasize Jesus as a teacher, perhaps even as a philosopher since philosophers in antiquity often discussed matters of great importance with their students while eating and drinking. We have examples of such dinner settings in the lives of Plato and Aristotle, two of the best-known philosophers of the ancient world. In settings such as these, it was considered an honor to sit at the feet of the teacher. Servants, however, busied themselves with preparing the meals while the teacher and his students talked.

However, this story in Luke is unlike most dinner settings, for Mary, a woman, was permitted to sit at Jesus's feet and listen to His teaching. The culture of the day—both Jewish as well as Gentile—did not think a woman should be taught or be with men (there were a few exceptions, but not many). One rabbi was remembered to have said, "Better to burn the Law of Moses than to teach it to a woman!" Contrary to this widely held thinking, Jesus saw no problem in teaching women.

Although the combination of the Jewish names "Martha" and "Mary" isn't unique (after all, we find these two names inscribed together in burial settings in Jerusalem), it is probable that the Mary and Martha of this story are the same women mentioned in the Gospel of John. There, we learn that Lazarus, the man Jesus raised up, was their brother (see John 11:1, 5, 21) and that Jesus stayed with the family of Mary, Martha, and Lazarus at the beginning of Passover week. (John 12:2–3).

Martha's frustration with her sister, Mary, is completely understandable. Anyone bustling about with meal preparations, making sure everyone is tended to, will sympathize with Martha—and probably share her annoyance with Mary. After all, women were expected to be tasked with meal preparation, not sitting and listening to men discussing theology.

But Jesus was no ordinary teacher. His theology was not ordinary either. Jesus was one of a kind; He was special, and His ministry was utterly unique. Mary sensed this and chose to sit and listen. This is why Jesus gently instructed the complaining Martha, "Mary has chosen the good part, which shall not be taken away from her" (verse 42). To be sure, Mary, like her sister Martha, could have served Jesus and the disciples, and the memory of the occasion would have given her joy. But listening carefully to Jesus and absorbing all that He taught would be far more memorable and enriching. This deep experience could never be taken from her.

In the context of the Gospel of Luke, where the evangelist is keen to show how Jesus's teaching compares to the teaching of Moses, it is probable that our story illustrates the great truth of Deuteronomy 8:3, "Man shall not live by bread alone." On that occasion in her home, Mary perceived that truth and acted upon it.

KEY TAKEAWAY

Nothing can take the place of time spent with God. All of us need moments when we can draw close to God, to His Word, and to the example of His Son. It might be no more than taking a few minutes to pray, to read a passage of Scripture, or to speak a word of encouragement to someone who is struggling. Yet, so often, we let the busyness of life and even Christian service compete with these moments, pushing us toward other things, things we believe are more urgent. "Another time," we think—time and time again, missing those opportunities to make time with God a priority.

THE STORY OF

the Parable of the Rich Man and His Bigger Barns

Jesus Teaches an Inheritance Is Shared

MAIN CHARACTERS

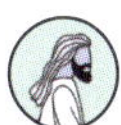
JESUS encounters a man who asks Him to mediate a family inheritance dispute.

A MAN wants Jesus to tell his brother to divide the inheritance with him.

THE DISCIPLES were likely present during this encounter, even though they are not explicitly mentioned.

A CROWD, along with the disciples, listens as Jesus tells a parable warning against investing one's life in the pursuit of wealth.

SCRIPTURE REFERENCE

Someone in the crowd said to Him, "Teacher, tell my brother to divide the family inheritance with me." But He said to him, "Man, who appointed Me a judge or arbitrator over you?" Then He said . . ., "Beware, and be on your guard against every form of greed; for not even when one has an abundance does his life consist of his possessions." And He told them a parable, saying, "The land of a rich man was very productive. And he began reasoning to himself, . . . 'What shall I do, since I have no place to store my crops?' Then he said, 'This is what I will do: I will tear down my barns and build larger ones, and . . . store all my grain and my goods. And I will say to my soul, "Soul, you have many goods laid up for many years . . .; take your ease, eat, drink, and be merry."' But God said to him, 'You fool! This very night your soul is required of you; and now who will own what you have prepared?' So is the man who stores up treasure for himself, and is not rich toward God." (Luke 12:13–21)

What You Might Assume

The man who approached Jesus was obsessed with material possessions and, therefore, should be faulted.

Jesus had no interest in material means; money and property meant nothing to Him.

Jesus was critical of the wealthy for simply being wealthy.

What Is More Likely

!

The man's concerns over a fair division of the family inheritance was a legitimate concern.

Jesus certainly did view money and stewardship as important, but He cautioned followers not to be controlled by materialism and the cares of the world.

Jesus was critical of the wealthy and not-so-wealthy alike when they placed their faith in their possessions.

The Story Behind the Scriptures

In the days of Jesus, one's livelihood and future security often depended on inheritance. The matter was so important that Old Testament law speaks to it (e.g., Deuteronomy 21:15–17). When the man comes to Jesus and asks Him to instruct his brother to share the inheritance, we probably have an instance where an older brother has inherited the lion's share of the estate and is unwilling to break up the farm. The brother who possesses the inheritance has probably told his brother to wait, and the brother is tired of waiting.

To the man's surprise, Jesus has no interest in acting as an arbitrator. Why? For two reasons at least: One, Israel in Jesus's time had courts, and local synagogues often acted as places of arbitration. Jesus had no need to play such a role. We might also suspect that the matter had been arbitrated, and the man was not happy with the outcome. The second reason is that for Jesus to take part in such a dispute would have redefined His ministry and message. Jesus taught His disciples to be generous and giving, not avaricious and grasping.

The exchange with the man gives Jesus the opportunity to tell a parable that illustrates the folly of measuring one's life in terms of one's wealth and of spending all one's life focused on oneself. The parable itself is easy to understand, but its lesson eludes us all almost on a daily basis. We can pile up a huge amount of money, supposing that we are now set for life, and then life comes to an end.

When this life ends, and we stand before God, there will be no interest in how much money we leave behind. Instead, the test of our hearts will be in what kind of life we have lived. Have we laid up treasure in heaven (Matthew 6:19–21)? Or, is all our treasure left behind on earth?

What's particularly interesting in the parable is what the wealthy man says to himself: "Soul, you have many goods laid up for many years to come; take it easy, eat, drink, and be merry" (verse 19). The phrase "eat, drink, and be merry" is often thought to have come from the Epicureans, a group of philosophers who believed in enjoying life rather than focusing on fasting or humility. They believed their gods didn't care much about human affairs, and it's sometimes assumed that Jesus was quoting them here. However, the expression appears several times in the Bible long before the Epicureans. King Solomon quotes it as he grapples with the meaning of life (Ecclesiastes 8:15), and it is quoted in Isaiah 22:13 as well. Centuries later, the apostle Paul quotes Isaiah as he argues that if there is no resurrection of the righteous (and Paul believes there truly is), then we may as well subscribe to the philosophy, "Let us eat and drink, for tomorrow we die" (I Corinthians 15:32).

Like many of those to whom Paul is speaking, the implication of the rich man's assumptions in the parable is that there is no life to come; there is no judgment. However, there is, and we are wise to plan for it.

KEY TAKEAWAY

We live in a very materialistic age, at a level of comfort and security never before experienced in the history of humanity. Yet, this prosperity can turn our hearts away from God. It can lead us to say to ourselves, "Take it easy; you have it made. Eat, drink, and enjoy life!" Jesus is not implying that we should not save enough money to look after ourselves but that we balance good stewardship of our possessions with serving God and others during our lives, and never forget that the day will come when we stand before God.

THE STORY OF

Healing the Woman with a Crooked Spine

Jesus Heals the Woman with a Crooked Spine

MAIN CHARACTERS

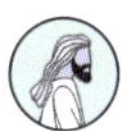
JESUS attends a synagogue service and heals a woman who is bent over and unable to stand upright.

A WOMAN, bent over and unable to stand upright, seeks healing from Jesus.

A SYNAGOGUE OFFICIAL criticizes Jesus for healing someone on the Sabbath day.

THE CROWD gathered in the synagogue witnesses the healing of the woman.

SCRIPTURE REFERENCE.

And He (Jesus) was teaching in one of the synagogues on the Sabbath. And there was a woman who for eighteen years had had a sickness caused by a spirit; and she was bent double, and could not straighten up at all. When Jesus saw her, He called her over and said to her, "Woman, you are freed from your sickness." And He laid His hands on her; and immediately she was made erect again and began glorifying God. But the synagogue official, indignant because Jesus had healed on the Sabbath, began saying to the crowd in response, "There are six days in which work should be done; so come during them and get healed, and not on the Sabbath day." But the Lord answered him and said, "You hypocrites, does not each of you on the Sabbath untie his ox or his donkey from the stall and lead him away to water him? And this woman, a daughter of Abraham as she is, whom Satan has bound for eighteen long years, should she not have been released from this bond on the Sabbath day?" As He said this, all His opponents were being humiliated; and the entire crowd was rejoicing over all the glorious things being done by Him. (Luke 13:10-17)

What You Might Assume

?

People gathered in synagogues only on the Sabbath (i.e., Saturdays).

The woman who was bent over was possessed by an evil spirit.

The synagogue official's complaint was entirely unjustified, and he had no compassion for the afflicted woman.

Jesus's opponents were utterly blind in their failure to appreciate the healing of the woman on the Sabbath.

What Is More Likely

People gathered in synagogues on other days of the week; mention of the Sabbath in the present story was necessary because of the controversy Jesus's healing created.

People assumed the woman's unfortunate condition was caused by an evil spirit, but it may be true that no literal spirit was present.

The synagogue official saw no reason for Jesus to heal the afflicted woman on the Sabbath; she could be healed the next day!

Jesus's opponents were not entirely unreasonable in raising questions about the healing of the woman—they needed to hear more from Jesus!

The Story Behind the Scriptures

In our story, we hear of a woman who was "bent double" and could not straighten herself. Interpreters today wonder if she had scoliosis, a sideways curvature of the spine, or (more likely) spondylitis ankylopoetica, a fusion of the vertebrae. In either case, the poor woman was disfigured and unable to stand straight, and she probably suffered a great deal. To make matters worse, many in her village thought her condition was "caused by a spirit," for it was widely believed that certain ailments, such as blindness and epilepsy, were caused by evil spirits. So not only was the woman physically disabled, she was thought to be possessed! However, it is probable that the evangelist Luke was only reporting what people assumed. After all, Jesus did not command the "spirit" to depart, as was always done in cases of exorcism. On the other hand, Jesus did refer to Satan, so people may have understood that even if a literal demon was not involved, Satan is the ultimate source of much of human suffering.

Jesus said, "Woman, you are freed from your sickness," and He laid His hands on her, and she was instantly healed and began to praise God. But the joy of the moment was quashed by an indignant leader of the synagogue: "There are six days in which work should be done; so come during them and get healed, and not on the Sabbath day," he said. The man had a point. After all, the woman's life was not in danger, so to wait one more day for healing wouldn't have been that big of a problem. Furthermore, the leader of the synagogue was reminding Jesus, the woman, and everyone in earshot that respect for the Sabbath was commanded in Scripture. One wasn't supposed to go about his daily work routine as though the Sabbath was just an ordinary day.

People were allowed to do things on the Sabbath. You could get out of bed, eat your breakfast, and walk to the synagogue. You could feed and care for your animals, too—untying them, leading them to water, and so on. In other contexts, Jesus reminded His critics that even on the Sabbath the Jewish people were allowed to go to a lot of trouble to help an animal that had fallen into a well (Matthew 12:11–12). If one can "work" to save the life of an animal, why was it wrong to help a human being—whose life is infinitely more valuable than the life of an animal—on the Sabbath? Did not Jesus say, "The Sabbath was made for man, and not man for the Sabbath" (Mark 2:27)?

But more importantly, if God heals someone (and that is what has happened—through Jesus, God healed the afflicted woman), then how can anyone say that the Sabbath law has been broken? A woman bound by Satan for many years was liberated. Isn't the Sabbath—the day of rest—the perfect day for such a wonderful event? Isn't this something to be celebrated? The crowd got the point, and they rejoiced.

KEY TAKEAWAY

Frequently in Jesus's teachings the emphasis falls on priorities. In the story above, the synagogue official was not wrong for respecting the Sabbath. In his time, that was very important. But he lost sight of the importance of the physical and spiritual health of a human being. He also lost sight of the true significance of the Sabbath—it was supposed to be a day of rest and freedom, not a day that binds and holds back. We, too, can get so caught up in how we think things should be done that we lose sight of the bigger purpose and deny blessings to ourselves and to others.

THE STORY OF

Healing the Canaanite Woman's Daughter

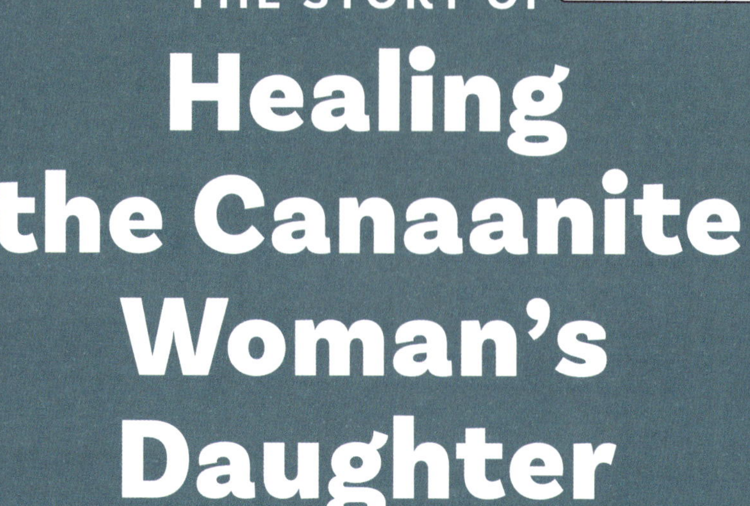

A Gentile Woman's Great Faith

MAIN CHARACTERS

JESUS journeys into the district of Tyre and Sidon, located northwest of Galilee.

A GENTILE WOMAN of Canaanite origins, desperate for help, appeals to Jesus on behalf of her daughter.

THE DISCIPLES of Jesus, annoyed by the woman's persistent pleas, urge Him to send her away.

SCRIPTURE REFERENCE

Jesus went away from there, and withdrew into the district of Tyre and Sidon. And a Canaanite woman from that region came out and began to cry out, saying, "Have mercy on me, Lord, Son of David; my daughter is cruelly demon-possessed." But He did not answer her a word. And His disciples came and implored Him, saying, "Send her away, because she keeps shouting at us." But He answered and said, "I was sent only to the lost sheep of the house of Israel." But she came and began to bow down before Him, saying, "Lord, help me!" And He answered and said, "It is not good to take the children's bread and throw it to the dogs." But she said, "Yes, Lord; but even the dogs feed on the crumbs which fall from their masters' table." Then Jesus said to her, "O woman, your faith is great; it shall be done for you as you wish." And her daughter was healed at once. (Matthew 15:21–28)

What You Might Assume

?

Jesus was surprisingly indifferent to the Gentile woman's distress. He always responded to those who appealed to Him. Why not this time?

Jesus insulted the Gentile woman, implying that she and all Gentiles were "dogs" unworthy of the bread of life.

The woman "changed" Jesus's mind, perhaps even corrected His thinking about the place of Gentiles in His ministry.

What Is More Likely

Jesus remained focused on His ministry, which focused first on the spiritual needs of Israel.

Jesus was only using an analogy about who is fed first—the children at the table and then later the dogs who feed upon the leftover scraps; He didn't insult the woman.

Jesus did what the Gentile woman asked because she responded in faith—the same kind of faith Jesus is looking for in His people.

The Story Behind the Scriptures

The story of Jesus's encounter with the Gentile woman is remarkable in many ways, from Jesus's initial refusal to hear her pleas to His commendation of her faith. Especially odd to our ears is His explanation for not initially offering her help: The children's bread wasn't to be thrown to "dogs." What did that mean? Did Jesus insult the woman because she was a Gentile?

Some early hearers of this story may well have assumed that Jesus put this woman in her place. She was a Gentile, but even worse in Jewish eyes, she was a Canaanite. The Canaanites—driven from Israel, the land God promised Abraham—were viewed very negatively in the Old Testament.

The biggest mystery in our story revolves around the references to bread and crumbs. When Jesus spoke of the "children's bread," He was referring to the great eschatological banquet promised by the prophet Isaiah in 25:6, when God Himself will treat His people to choice food and drink. In one of the stories in the Gospel of Luke, a man cries out, "Blessed is everyone who will eat bread in the kingdom of God!" (Luke 14:15). That's the bread Jesus was talking about.

To make His point, Jesus used the illustration of a typical meal: The members of the household are served first. After they eat, leftover scraps are thrown to the dogs outside. We see this in the parable of the rich man and Lazarus in Luke 16:21. But here is where our story gets interesting. Because Jesus referred to the people of Israel as "children" (which was common), the Gentile woman, taking "children" literally, spoke of the dogs beneath the table eating the "crumbs which fall from their masters' table." (Anyone who has had young children sitting at the table knows there will be plenty of crumbs on the floor!) The woman built on Jesus's illustration. Yes, the children are first to eat the food, and yes, the scraps of food will be thrown to the dogs outside, but crumbs do fall from the table while the children are eating, and the little indoor dogs eat those crumbs. The woman was implying that even a tiny crumb from Jesus would be more than enough to meet her needs. Also, the response of

Jesus to the woman implied that the time of salvation would also come for the Gentiles.

In saying this, the woman expressed great faith. Jesus was very impressed: "O woman, your faith is great; it shall be done for you as you wish." The woman didn't contradict or correct Jesus; she agreed with Him. Her expression of faith was very much in step with Jesus's call for repentance and faith in the good news of what God was doing through Him and His ministry. The woman's expression of faith and the resultant healing of her daughter anticipate the mission of the Church, where the people in Phoenicia—where the cities of Tyre and Sidon are located—are converted (see Acts 15:3).

KEY TAKEAWAY

Once we understand the culture and imagery behind the story of Jesus's encounter with the Gentile woman from the district of Tyre and Sidon, we are able to see that it is not a story about racism but about the importance of faith and Jesus's generous benevolence to all. The story of the Gentile woman is preserved in the Gospels because this woman exemplifies the kind of faith Jesus is seeking. Do we have this kind of faith in Jesus?

THE STORY OF

the Great Banquet and Who Will Enjoy It

Jesus Attends the Dinner Banquet

MAIN CHARACTERS

JESUS, who has been invited to dinner, probably received the invitation after His visit to a village where He did some teaching.

THE HOST, an official and a member of the conservative religious group known as the Pharisees (see Luke 14:1), invited Jesus to dinner.

ONE OF THE GUESTS at the dinner, perhaps sensing tension, pronounces a blessing on all who eat bread in God's kingdom (see Luke 14:15).

SEVERAL GUESTS at the dinner, eager to learn more about Jesus and His message, listen closely to His words.

SCRIPTURE REFERENCE

But He (Jesus) said to him, "A man was giving a big dinner, and he invited many; and at the dinner hour he sent his slave to say to those who had been invited, 'Come; for everything is ready now.' But they all alike began to make excuses. The first one said to him, 'I have bought a piece of land and I need to go out and look at it; please consider me excused.' Another one said, 'I have bought five yoke of oxen, and I am going to try them out; please consider me excused.' Another one said, 'I have married a wife, and for that reason I cannot come.' And the slave came back and reported this to his master. Then the head of the household became angry and said to his slave, 'Go out at once into the streets and lanes of the city and bring in here the poor and crippled and blind and lame.' And the slave said, 'Master, what you commanded has been done, and still there is room.' And the master said to the slave, 'Go out into the highways and along the hedges, and compel them to come in, so that my house may be filled. For I tell you, none of those men who were invited shall taste of my dinner.'" (Luke 14:16–24)

What You Might Assume

The parable is about rude guests who should have informed their generous host sooner that they would be unable to join him for supper.

The parable warns about the dangers of wealth.

Poverty and poor health are signs of divine displeasure.

The poor and crippled are more deserving of God's grace than are the healthy and wealthy.

What Is More Likely

!

The parable really isn't about rude guests at all but is about those who assume their entry into the kingdom of God is a sure thing.

The parable warns about assuming one's blessings are sure signs of God's approval when, in fact, they may not be at all.

Poverty and poor health are not indicators of God's displeasure.

No one is more deserving than another; the point is that often the poor and disadvantaged are more open to what God offers.

The Story Behind the Scriptures

The story of the banquet is full of awkward moments. Jesus "went into the house of one of the leaders of the Pharisees on the Sabbath" to eat dinner (Luke 14:1). Because it was the Sabbath day when Jesus received this invitation, we should assume that He had preached in the local synagogue and that His host was a leader of the synagogue. As was the case earlier in His ministry (see Luke 7:36–50), Jesus was probably invited to dinner out of a sense of obligation, not necessarily out of admiration or respect. Before the dinner got underway and probably before Jesus entered His host's house, He encountered a "man suffering from dropsy" (Luke 14:2). Even though it was the Sabbath, when one was not supposed to work, Jesus healed the man and scolded His critics: "Which one of you will have a son or an ox fall into a well, and will not immediately pull him out on a Sabbath day?" Jesus had made a similar point before (see Luke 13:15).

When the dinner got underway, Jesus noted how people chose the places of honor around the table (Luke 14:7). He suggested they show some humility and not presume that the best seats were reserved for them (14:8–11, alluding to Proverbs 25:6–7). Jesus then suggested that His affluent host and others like him invite the poor to their dinner parties, rather than the wealthy, who would reciprocate (Luke 14:12–14). After all, it is not generous to invite people to dinner who will then invite you to dinner. By now, we may imagine, the host and his guests were becoming annoyed with their celebrated guest.

To break the tension, one of the guests pronounced a blessing on all who will eat bread in God's kingdom (14:15). As in the story considered earlier (see the previous lesson on Matthew 15:21–28), eating bread in the kingdom anticipates the great messianic feast promised in Isaiah 25:6. The Jewish men of Qumran near the Dead Sea (writers and collectors of the famous Dead Sea Scrolls) anticipated a time when the righteous will sit at table with the Messiah and enjoy a great feast. But because of their commitment to purity, the men of Qumran (and probably most contemporaries of Jesus) believed that the blemished and disabled would not be allowed to sit at the table with the Messiah. Jesus didn't see it that way.

In His parable, Jesus warns that health and wealth are not sure signs that one's relationship with God is secure. Indeed, one's wealth can become a distraction. When God summons us, we might say, "Sorry, but I have something important that needs attention." In contrast, the poor and infirm, thought by some to be sinners far from God, might be quick to answer God's summons. Jesus's parable suggests that not only will the poor of Israel respond to the invitation to enter the kingdom, but Gentiles (i.e., those out in "the highways and along the hedges") will also.

KEY TAKEAWAY

It is true that Scripture teaches that if God's people are obedient, they will be blessed, and if they are disobedient, they will be judged (and this is clearly taught in the book of Deuteronomy). But Jesus teaches that material wealth is not necessarily a sign of God's blessing, any more than poverty and ill health are signs of God's displeasure. Whether we find ourselves in abundance or in want, the lesson of the parable is for us to say yes to God.

THE STORY OF

the Parable of the Prodigal Son

Jesus Tells the Parable of the Prodigal Son

MAIN CHARACTERS

JESUS spends time teaching and eating with people who are viewed as dubious, if not outcasts from polite society.

THE PEOPLE Jesus interacts with are often referred to as "sinners," typically because they do not follow the Law of Moses as strictly as some religious teachers believe it should be followed.

THE PHARISEES AND SCRIBES, who claim to keep the Law of Moses perfectly (or at least think they do), often clash with Jesus over His teachings and actions.

SCRIPTURE REFERENCE

"A man had two sons. The younger of them said to his father, 'Father, give me athe share of the estate that falls to me.' So he divided his wealth between them. And not many days later, the younger son gathered everything together and went on a journey into a distant country, and there he squandered his estate with loose living. Now when he had spent everything, a severe famine occurred in that country, and he began to be impoverished. So he went and hired himself out to one of the citizens of that country, and he sent him into his fields to feed swine. And he would have gladly filled his stomach with the pods that the swine were eating, and no one was giving anything to him. But when he came to his senses, he said, 'How many of my father's hired men have more than enough bread, but I am dying here with hunger! I will get up and go to my father, and will say to him, "Father, I have sinned against heaven, and in your sight; I am no longer worthy to be called your son; make me as one of your hired men."' So he got up and came to his father. But while he was still a long way off, his father saw him and felt compassion for him, and ran and embraced him and kissed him. And the son said to him, 'Father, I have sinned against heaven and in your sight; I am no longer worthy to be called your son.' But the father said to his slaves, 'Quickly bring out the best robe and put it on him, and put a ring on his hand and sandals on his feet; and bring the fattened calf, kill it, and let us eat and celebrate; for this son of mine was dead and has come to life again; he was lost and has been found.' And they began to celebrate." (Luke 15:11–24)

What You Might Assume

The "sinners" (see Luke 15:1) with whom Jesus was associating were actually decent people; their only "sin" was a failure to keep some of the technicalities of the Law of Moses.

The Pharisees and scribes, who were concerned about the company Jesus kept, were all hypocrites.

The man of the parable couldn't have had too much trouble dividing his estate between his two sons.

It really wasn't wrong for the younger son to ask for his share of his inheritance.

The father's response to the return of the prodigal was reasonable and expected.

What Is More Likely

!

The "sinners" listening to Jesus really were sinful, or at least some of them were. They probably included tax collectors, prostitutes, drunks, and thieves.

The Pharisees and scribes were, for the most part, pious, Law-observant people who sincerely believed God would bless the nation of Israel if the Jewish people kept the Law.

In an ancient agrarian culture, dividing up property was very difficult; there were no bank accounts or stock that could be sold.

Ancient Jewish society would have viewed the younger son's request for his inheritance to be very disrespectful, and for his father to comply would be reckless.

Most people hearing this parable don't see the father's response as reasonable; rather, much too forgiving.

The Story Behind the Scriptures

The parable of the Prodigal Son is a classic, and it's not hard to see why. Almost every family has experienced something like it and so can readily identify with it. The parable portrays a young fool who has dishonored his father and family, squandered his inheritance in sinful, reckless living, finds himself in deplorable circumstances, and then finally comes to his senses. He returns home, repents, and is forgiven.

The parable is told while Jesus is teaching and eating with social outcasts, referred to as "sinners." Once again, the Pharisees and teachers of the law couldn't believe that Jesus would spend so much time receiving and eating with such people. Jesus tells three parables to defend His involvement with the lost and reveal God's attitude.

If the parable of the Prodigal Son was read through the lens of the culture of Israel of old, we would be shocked at the young man's behavior. To ask for his share of the family farm (which would be one-third of the estate—see Deuteronomy 21:15–17) while his father still lived would have been viewed as disrespectful. To sell off his portion, gather up his money, and then leave his family would have been viewed as apostasy (and, indeed, the lad travels to a Gentile land where Israel's ancient faith was not observed). To waste his inheritance on wild living and prostitutes would have been viewed as unforgivable, especially to become so desperate in his poverty that he agrees to work for a Gentile feeding swine (an unclean animal for Jews)!

When he finally repents, the young man returns home expecting at most to become a hired servant. But his father forgives him, celebrates his return ("return" in the Old Testament means "repentance"), and restores the lad fully to his place in the family. The father also assures his older son, who has always been faithful, that in regaining his lost brother he has lost nothing (see Luke 15:25–32).

All who hear this parable understand it. The "sinners" who are eating with Jesus know that the foolish younger son represents them. Like this fool, they have abandoned faith and family. Now they are being invited to return. The older son represents the murmuring Pharisees and scribes (see Luke 15:2). Jesus has not insulted the religious leaders, and neither has He paid a compliment to the sinners who have gathered around him. Rather, He has invited them all to come together, to be reconciled as brothers and sisters.

KEY TAKEAWAY

The parable of the Prodigal Son teaches that no matter how deep into sin and degradation one has fallen, forgiveness is still possible. Relationship with God can be restored; in fact, God has been patiently waiting for us and will welcome us back with open arms. But there is more: As God forgives the sinner, we, too, must forgive. When the lost are found (that is, when they repent), it is cause for rejoicing.

THE STORY OF

the Parable of the Unrighteous Judge and Persistent Widow

Jesus Teaches about God's Righteous Judgment

MAIN CHARACTERS

JESUS, who is approaching Jerusalem, has been warning His followers of the approaching day of judgment.

A JUDGE in Jesus' parable is described as having no commitment to justice and no regard for God or man.

A WIDOW is portrayed as someone who, with untiring persistence, demands justice.

SCRIPTURE REFERENCE

Now He (Jesus) was telling them a parable to show that at all times they ought to pray and not to lose heart, saying, "In a certain city there was a judge who did not fear God and did not respect man. There was a widow in that city, and she kept coming to him, saying, 'Give me legal protection from my opponent.' For a while he was unwilling; but afterward he said to himself, 'Even though I do not fear God nor respect man, yet because this widow bothers me, I will give her legal protection, otherwise by continually coming she will wear me out.'" And the Lord said, "Hear what the unrighteous judge said; now, will not God bring about justice for His elect who cry to Him day and night, and will He delay long over them? I tell you that He will bring about justice for them quickly." (Luke 18:1–8)

What You Might Assume

?

Comparing God to an unrighteous human judge is inappropriate.

The widow enjoyed financial support and judicial protection (as spelled out in the Law of Moses)

The human judge was incompetent.

Pestering God with repetitive prayers is what we need to do.

What Is More Likely

!

The point of comparing God with an unrighteous human judge is to underscore the contrast between God, who cares for people, and a human judge who doesn't.

The widow probably received very little financial support and judicial protection.

The human judge catered to the wealthy and the powerful; to him, the widow was nobody.

We do not need repetitive prayers because God cares about us and hears us the first time.

The Story Behind the Scriptures

To make His point that God's people should never lose hope but always pray, Jesus told a parable of the unrighteous judge and persistent widow. Hearers of this parable would have no problem imagining a corrupt judge who favored the wealthy and powerful and ignored the poor and powerless. Jewish hearers who know Scripture would immediately think of the Law of Moses, where Israel is commanded to appoint men who will judge righteously (e.g., Deuteronomy 1:16; 17:18). Jehoshaphat the righteous king of Judah admonished the judges of his day: "Consider what you are doing, for you do not judge for man but for the Lord who is with you when you render judgment. Now then let the fear of the Lord be upon you; be very careful what you do, for the Lord our God will have no part in unrighteousness or partiality vor the taking of a bribe" (II Chronicles 19:6–7). The judge in Jesus's parable does not exemplify the commands of the Law of Moses or the charge given by King Jehoshaphat. The corrupt judge of the parable has no respect for God or for humanity.

The ultimate righteous Judge, of course, is God Himself. The Psalms declare, "God is a righteous judge" (Psalm 7:11) who "will judge the world in righteousness" and "will execute judgment for the peoples with equity (Psalm 9:8).

Old Testament Scripture also commands people to care for widows and orphans. God commands, "You shall not afflict any widow or orphan" (Exodus 22:22). God Himself "executes justice for the orphan and the widow" (Deuteronomy 10:18). The widow and orphan are to be provided food (Deuteronomy 14:29; cf. 16:14; 28:12) and allowed to glean in the fields, orchards, and vineyards (Deuteronomy 24:19–21). He who obstructs justice for the widow or orphan is under God's curse (Deuteronomy 27:19).

The unrighteous judge of Jesus's parable applies none of these commands to himself; he utterly ignores them. He is above the law. He is a law to himself. He privileges the wealthy and the powerful, all to his own benefit. The unrighteous judge of the parable exemplifies none of the integrity that God expects. He has no respect for God and thus cares nothing for justice. As for the widow and her complaint, he has no concern whatsoever.

Yet, the widow secures righteous judgment for herself because of her persistence. The uncaring, unrighteous judge gives in to her persistent appeals, saying to himself, "I will give her legal protection, otherwise by continually coming she will wear me out." And, of course, this is exactly where the judge of the parable differs from God, the ultimate and final Judge of all. The corrupt human judge renders just judgment because the widow wears him out; God will render fair and righteous judgment for his people because He loves them. God does not need to be badgered; He is the kind of Judge people should go to with their prayers and petitions.

Jews listening to Jesus understand the logic of His parable, for it follows the reasoning of the Jewish teachers of that time: If something is true in a lesser or more unlikely case, it will certainly be true in a greater or more likely case. Applied to the parable, it means that if a corrupt judge eventually gives justice, then surely God, a righteous Judge, will do so.

KEY TAKEAWAY

Jesus teaches us to pray and not to lose heart because God is a righteous Judge and loves His people. It is easy to lose heart, for we are often impatient. We want results now. But God knows timing better than we do. If He delays in answering our prayers, it is not because He doesn't care or needs to be nagged! It is because He knows what is needed and when it is right.

THE STORY OF

the Parable of the Self-Righteous Pharisee and the Repentant Tax Collector

Jesus Compares Two Prayers and Two Heart Postures

MAIN CHARACTERS

JESUS, who is approaching Jerusalem, where Israel's beautiful temple is located, teaches His disciples and crowds concerning what constitutes true faith.

TWO MEN are featured in Jesus's parable, with the first being a self-righteous Pharisee, a man who believes his service to God is almost flawless.

THE SECOND MAN in Jesus's parable is a repentant tax collector who begs for God's mercy.

SCRIPTURE REFERENCE

And He [Jesus] also told this parable to some people who trusted in themselves that they were righteous, and viewed others with contempt: "Two men went up into the temple to pray, one a Pharisee and the other a tax collector. The Pharisee stood and was praying this to himself: 'God, I thank You that I am not like other people: swindlers, unjust, adulterers, or even like this tax collector. I fast twice a week; I pay tithes of all that I get.' But the tax collector, standing some distance away, was even unwilling to lift up his eyes to heaven, but was beating his breast, saying, 'God, be merciful to me, the sinner!' I tell you, this man went to his house justified rather than the other; for everyone who exalts himself will be humbled, but he who humbles himself will be exalted." (Luke 18:9–14)

What You Might Assume

All Pharisees were self-righteous hypocrites who saw themselves as the only ones who understood the Law of Moses properly.

All tax and toll collectors were greedy, dishonest cheats.

Praying out loud was always for show.

The Pharisee's prayer was entirely self-congratulatory and a chance for him to boast of his piety.

What Is More Likely

!

Not all Pharisees were self-righteous hypocrites (and to be self-righteous, one did not need to be a Pharisee), but the Pharisee of the parable certainly was.

Some tax and toll collectors were dishonest, true, but not all were; even the worst of the lot sometimes repented, as does the man in the parable.

Praying out loud was a common practice in antiquity; praying silently was rare.

The Pharisee went up to the temple to pray what Deuteronomy 26 requires of all Jewish men; unfortunately his presumption turned the prayer into a boast.

The Story Behind the Scriptures

This parable is really the parable of two prayers and two kinds of hearts. The Pharisee is praying as he has been taught in Deuteronomy 26, where Moses instructs the Israelites on how they should go up to the holy place where the tabernacle (and later the temple) would be and offer up specific prayers of thanks to God for His many blessings. (Deuteronomy 26:8–10).

It is a beautiful prayer of thanksgiving and gratitude. No doubt most Jews who went up to the temple and spoke these words meant them sincerely. But there was the temptation to turn the prayer into boasting and self-congratulation. We hear this lack of humility in the prayer of the parable's Pharisee, who thanks God that he is "not like other people: swindlers, unjust, adulterers, or even like this tax collector." What he is really saying is, "God, you don't know how lucky You are to have me!"

In Jesus's day, tax collectors were despised. Not only were they viewed as dishonest, but they were also viewed as traitors who worked for Herod and his sons or for the Romans. Unpopular and distrusted, tax collectors are often lumped in with sinners (Matthew 9:11; 11:19).

It's hard for us to imagine standing in church or anywhere and loudly praying our deepest thoughts out loud, seemingly drawing attention to ourselves. However, in Jesus's day, silent prayer was not at all the norm, and it was expected that these men would loudly call out to God. It's not hard to understand how someone who lacked humility might be tempted to boast aloud. When in His parable, Jesus mentioned a tax collector going up to the temple to pray, we should assume that some of the hearers scoffed, perhaps muttering, "What tax collector ever went up to the temple to pray?" Or even, "How pathetic!"

The Pharisee who went up to the temple to pray presumed that he was righteous and that God was pleased with him. The tax collector presumed no such thing. Instead, he begs God for mercy, confessing that he is a "sinner." Unlike the Pharisee, who showily lifts up his hands and looks to heaven for all to see, the tax collector hangs his head in shame and beats his breast. He may not realize it, but he is the one who has truly grasped the significance of the prayer commanded in Deuteronomy 26. In his repentance and confession as a sinner, the tax collector acknowledged that it was in God's mercy and compassion that the people of Israel were blessed, not because they deserved it.

The parable ends on an unexpected note: It was the tax collector, *not the Pharisee*, who went home righteous in the eyes of God.

KEY TAKEAWAY

How easy it is for us to become smug. We often judge others by externals, having no idea what is in their hearts. The beauty of Jesus's parable of the Pharisee and the tax collector is how it so clearly defines what true righteousness is and reminds us that the prayer God hears is the prayer from a humble and contrite heart—one that appreciates what God can give. It is not presumption, and it certainly is not running down others, who by appearance do not seem to fit our idea of those close to God. True righteousness comes from speaking the truth to God and letting Him work in us.

THE STORY OF

Raising Lazarus

Lazarus Has Been Dead "Four Days"

MAIN CHARACTERS

JESUS has traveled south into Judea and is now in the vicinity of the Jordan River to the east, where He and John the Baptist had been active in baptizing.

MARY of Bethany is the sister of Martha and Lazarus.

MARTHA of Bethany is the sister of Mary and Lazarus.

THE NEIGHBORS who live in Bethany know the family of Mary, Martha, and Lazarus.

LAZARUS of Bethany, the brother of Mary and Martha, was gravely ill and has now died.

SCRIPTURE REFERENCE:

Jesus said to her, "Your brother will rise again." Martha said to Him, "I know that he will rise again in the resurrection on the last day." Jesus said to her, "I am the resurrection and the life; he who believes in Me will live even if he dies, and everyone who lives and believes in Me will never die. Do you believe this?" She said . . . , "I have believed that You are the Christ, the Son of God, who comes into the world." . . . Jesus said, "Remove the stone." Martha . . . said, "Lord, by this time there will be a stench, for he has been dead four days." Jesus said to her, "Did I not say to you that if you believe, you will see the glory of God?" So they removed the stone. Then Jesus raised His eyes, and said, "Father, I thank You that You have heard Me. I knew that You always hear Me; but because of the people standing around I said it, so that they may believe that You sent Me." . . . He cried out . . . , "Lazarus, come forth." The man who had died came forth. (John 11:23–27, 39–44)

What You Might Assume

Jesus was indifferent to the Bethany family's concerns, and because of His delay in making the journey from the Jordan River to Jerusalem, Jesus, in effect, let Lazarus die.

Perhaps Lazarus really wasn't dead, only comatose; he was only in need of being awakened.

The reference to "four days" conveyed no special meaning beyond the obvious.

Resurrection is essentially the same as resuscitation.

What Is More Likely

!

Jesus cared deeply about Lazarus and his sisters, and He knew Lazarus would soon pass away, but hope remained.

Lazarus truly died and remained dead for four days, which according to the Jewish understanding confirmed that the man had no hope of waking up.

The reference to “four days” meant the spirit of the deceased had truly departed and that new life could only come about through the resurrection.

The raising of Lazarus was not an instance of resurrection, which will take place in the future, but it was more than a mere resuscitation.

The Story Behind the Scriptures

Nothing is more final than death. A family member passes away, and a few days later we attend the funeral. We grieve. We console. We certainly do not expect to see that family member again in this life. During the ministry of Jesus, however, the unexpected often happened.

The story of the raising of Lazarus is quite dramatic on the face of it, but when Jewish beliefs and customs regarding burial are taken into account, the story takes on added significance. To understand this significance, it is important that we understand Jewish burial practices. In the time of Jesus, the Jewish people buried the dead the day of their death (and if death occurred just before the end of the day or in the night, burial took place the following day). The body was washed, perfumed, wrapped, and then carried out of the village to the place of burial. There the family mourned for seven days, either outside of the tomb or inside it. One year later, the family returned to the tomb to gather the bones and place them in a niche or in an ossuary (bone box).

When Lazarus, brother of Mary and Martha, died, we should assume that his family and friends followed these customs. The body of Lazarus was washed, perfumed, wrapped, and then placed in the family tomb. Four days later Jesus arrived and was told that Lazarus had died. His sisters were grieving. If only Jesus had arrived sooner, perhaps He could have healed Lazarus and he would still be living. But he was dead and wouldn't live again until the day of resurrection, occurring on Judgment Day. Jesus told the weeping Martha, "I am the resurrection and the life; he who believes in Me will live even if he dies, and everyone who lives and believes in Me will never die" (verses 25–26).

What Jesus claimed was astonishing. He wasn't simply affirming the truth of the resurrection that will occur someday; He claimed *to be the resurrection*. And to prove it, He would raise up Lazarus. "Lord, by this time there will be a stench, for he has been dead four days," Martha responded. What's so important about "four days"? Wouldn't you be just as dead if you had died two days ago? The point is that Jews believed the spirit of the deceased hovered near the body for three days, and then on the fourth day the spirit departed, thus leaving no hope of resuscitation. But for Jesus, no problem. He is the resurrection and the life, and He could raise Martha's brother, no matter how dead: "Lazarus, come forth!" (verse 43). And Lazarus did! Raising Lazarus, who was truly dead, foreshadowed the day of resurrection.

KEY TAKEAWAY

Because of the resurrection of Jesus, the apostle Paul can later confidently assert (quoting Isaiah 25:8), "Death is swallowed up in victory" and then ask with a note of mockery (quoting Hosea 13:14), "O Death, where is your victory? O Death, where is your sting?" (I Corinthians 15:54–55). In raising up Lazarus—dead for four days!—Jesus demonstrated His power over death and the truth of His amazing claim: "I am the resurrection and the life." No other truth gives us greater hope than this.

THE STORY OF

the Discovery of the Empty Tomb

Mary Magdalene Comes to the Tomb and Finds it Empty

MAIN CHARACTERS

MARY MAGDALENE, the most prominent of the women who follow Jesus, is the first to visit the tomb of Jesus early Sunday morning.

THE DISCIPLE PETER AND THE "OTHER DISCIPLE," whom Jesus loved, come to the tomb when they hear Mary's report.

JESUS, crucified and buried, has vanished, leaving behind His burial wrappings.

SCRIPTURE REFERENCE

Now on the first day of the week Mary Magdalene came early to the tomb, while it was still dark, and saw the stone already taken away from the tomb. So she ran and came to Simon Peter and to the other disciple whom Jesus loved, and said to them, 'They have taken away the Lord out of the tomb, and we do not know where they have laid Him.' So Peter and the other disciple went forth, and they were going to the tomb. The two were running together; and the other disciple ran ahead faster than Peter and came to the tomb first; and stooping and looking in, he saw the linen wrappings lying there; but he did not go in. And so Simon Peter also came, following him, and entered the tomb; and he saw the linen wrappings lying there, and the face-cloth which had been on His head, not lying with the linen wrappings, but rolled up in a place by itself. So the other disciple who had first come to the tomb then also entered, and he saw and believed. (John 20:1–8)

What You Might Assume

Mary Magdalene came to the tomb of Jesus early Sunday out of sorrow and perhaps also out of curiosity.

It would not be unusual for women to be recorded as credible eyewitnesses.

The tomb was an above-ground structure like a mausoleum.

The stone over the entrance was round.

The entrance to the tomb was a vertical opening, like a typical doorway.

What Is More Likely

Mary came to the tomb of Jesus to mourn and perhaps to augment the perfuming and anointing of Jesus's body.

Because it was rare that women were taken seriously as credible witnesses, the fact that a woman was recorded as the first witness points to the authenticity of the story.

The tomb was hewn out of the rock of a limestone terrace and was more like a cave.

Based on archaeological evidence, the stone door was likely a square block.

Visitors to the tomb had to stoop because their entrances were three-foot square openings close to the ground.

The Story Behind the Scriptures

Jesus died on a Friday, just before the Sabbath (Saturday), the day on which no Jew would be allowed to do the "work" of attending to the dead. Consequently, Mary came to the tomb on Sunday (the first day of the week). Jewish law and custom required the dead to be buried on the day of death before sundown. (In the case of death during the night, burial took place the following morning.) The body was washed, perfumed, wrapped with linen cloths, and placed in a tomb. These activities did not have to be completed the first day; they could be completed over a period of seven days as family members mourned at or even within the tomb.

One year later, the bones of the deceased were gathered and placed in a niche or in a bone box, which is called an ossuary. Sometimes the name of the deceased was inscribed on the box. In the case of those executed, public mourning was not permitted, nor was burial in the family tomb or any other place of honor. Rather, the deceased was placed in a tomb set aside for those executed. After one year, their bones could then be gathered and taken to the family tomb.

But with Jesus, things unfolded differently. Joseph of Arimathea, a disciple of Jesus, offered to have the body of Jesus placed in a tomb he had recently made (John 19:38). Because no corpse had been placed in this newly hewn tomb, it was not yet a "place of honor." Therefore, someone executed could be buried in it. This was very generous on the part of Joseph, for by placing the body of Jesus in this new tomb, it became a place of dishonor, thus rendering it useless to his family. The Gospel of John goes on to say that Nicodemus, who on a prior occasion had met with Jesus (see John 3), brought a large quantity of spices (John 19:39). He and Joseph then bound the body of Jesus "in linen wrapping with the spices, as is the burial custom of the Jews" (John 19:40).

When telling this story, all four Gospels say that women returned to the tomb early Sunday morning to anoint the body of Jesus. Either they did not know what Nicodemus had done, or they assumed that given how hurried they were the afternoon of Jesus's death, the process of washing and anointing had not been completed. Whatever the case, what the women didn't expect was to find the stone door of the tomb rolled aside and the body of Jesus gone.

The women assumed that the authorities had removed the body of Jesus and had taken it to one of the burial sites set aside for the executed. This is why Mary said to the disciples, "They have taken away the Lord out of the tomb, and we do not know where they have laid Him" (verse 2). Shocked, Peter and another disciple ran to the tomb and found it empty, just as Mary had said. But the tomb wasn't empty, not exactly. The disciples saw the linen wrappings and the face cloth (verse 7). If the authorities had removed the body of Jesus, they would not have unwrapped the body before removing it. When the "other disciple" saw these things, "he believed." He believed because it rightly dawned on him that the body of Jesus had not been *taken*; rather, Jesus had been *resurrected*, as He all along had said would happen.

KEY TAKEAWAY

The stunning discovery of the empty tomb is where, in a sense, the Christian faith had its beginning. To be sure, the amazing ministry of Jesus, complete with miracles and profound teaching, got the ball rolling, but it was His resurrection that was the game changer. Mary found the tomb empty, the disciples saw the linen wrappings, and then Jesus Himself appeared to Mary and the disciples—thus confirming the reality of the resurrection.

The Risen Jesus Meets the Men on the Road to Emmaus

MAIN CHARACTERS

JESUS, the risen One, has begun to show Himself alive to His disciples and family.

THE TWO DISCIPLES on the road to Emmaus are convinced that their mission to Israel, and ultimately the world, has come to a bitter end with the death of Jesus.

SCRIPTURE REFERENCE

And behold, two of them were going that very day to a village named Emmaus. . . . And they were talking with each other about all these things which had taken place. While they were talking and discussing, Jesus Himself approached and began traveling with them. But their eyes were prevented from recognizing Him. And He said to them, "What are these words that you are exchanging with one another as you are walking?" . . . And they said to Him, "The things about Jesus the Nazarene, who was a prophet mighty in deed and word in the sight of God and all the people, and how the chief priests and our rulers delivered Him to the sentence of death, and crucified Him. But we were hoping that it was He who was going to redeem Israel. Indeed, besides all this, it is the third day since these things happened. But also some women among us amazed us. When they were at the tomb early in the morning, and did not find His body, they came, saying that they had also seen a vision of angels who said that He was alive. Some of those who were with us went to the tomb and found it just exactly as the women also had said; but Him they did not see." And He said to them, "O foolish men and slow of heart to believe in all that the prophets have spoken! Was it not necessary for the Christ to suffer these things and to enter into His glory?" Then beginning with Moses and with all the prophets, He explained to them the things concerning Himself in all the Scriptures. (Luke 24:13–17, 19–27)

What You Might Assume

It was strange that the disciples did not recognize Jesus.

Surely the disciples knew that Jesus would be crucified and resurrected on the third day, just as He had predicted on several occasions during His ministry.

Surely the disciples knew the Scriptures that spoke of the Messiah's suffering and resurrection.

People understood the message of Jesus, that Roman rule over Israel would soon come to an end.

The discovery of the empty tomb should have immediately made plain to the disciples that Jesus had been raised from the dead.

What Is More Likely

The disciples did not recognize Jesus because He was transformed by His resurrection.

The disciples did not know that Jesus would be crucified. In fact, they hoped He wouldn't. As for the resurrection, the disciples assumed that it would take place someday in the future, not necessarily the following Sunday.

The disciples focused on prophecies that spoke of the Messiah's victory and enthronement, not His suffering and death.

By the time Jesus arrived at Jerusalem to celebrate the Passover, people held many opinions of Jesus and what He intended to accomplish.

Discovery of the empty tomb would have only added to the disciples' confusion as to what had happened to Jesus.

The Story Behind the Scriptures

When dramatic, unexpected things overtake us, it is only natural to be confused and frightened. We can hardly fault the followers of Jesus for not knowing what to make of the events of the Passover when their Master was arrested, put on trial, and then crucified. Then suddenly they were hearing reports that His body had gone missing and angels were making appearances! Could it get any more confusing?

When people began following Jesus, they hoped for major change in Israel and in the world. They longed for an end to Roman domination. They longed for an end to the corruption and oppressive temple establishment. And they longed for the fulfillment of the prophecies that promised a new earth and a new Jerusalem. What they didn't long for was the crucifixion of Jesus. After all, wasn't the Messiah supposed to reign forever (see John 12:34)?

The followers of Jesus knew, of course, that opposition and suffering were a possibility. They knew that persecution could come and that some of Jesus's followers might even die. They also believed in the resurrection of the righteous in the Day of Judgment that was someday coming. But the sudden death of Jesus during Passover was a shock—and mysterious reports of strange events at his place of burial only made things more confusing.

This is why it was so important that the risen Jesus met His disciples and explained to them from Scripture that what had happened fulfilled Scripture. "O foolish men and slow of heart to believe in all that the prophets have spoken!" (verse 25), Jesus tells the two disciples on the road to Emmaus. Jesus then opened their minds to the prophecies in the Old Testament that foretold the suffering, death, and resurrection of Jesus.

Also, Jesus wanted to make it clear that He was resurrected—it wasn't just some ghostly resuscitation. This is why, in a later passage in the Gospel of Luke (see Luke 24: 36–43), the risen Jesus again appeared to His disciples and ate food in their presence. What was the point of that? It was believed that angels and ghosts did not eat food. Only real, live human beings could eat. And Jesus was a real, live, resurrected human being. His disciples could touch Him and eat meals with Him. So they knew it really was Jesus, the Jesus with whom they had walked and talked. He was—and still is—alive!

KEY TAKEAWAY

The irreducible essence of Christian faith is the resurrection of Jesus (see I Corinthians 15). It was a real resurrection of the body. It is not a ghost story about the spirit of Jesus, which appears to people from time to time. It was the real Jesus, the Jesus the disciples knew well and with whom they had lived, who was raised up and appeared to them. Now they understood the Scriptures and knew that prophecy had been fulfilled. Their confusion was gone. In its place were joy and a new sense of mission. Thanks to the resurrection, we too can have this same joy, knowing that we are reconciled to God and that eternal life is not wishful thinking.

Wow Conclusion

We hope this little book has inspired you to go deeper into the Gospels. The thirty passages that we have looked at illustrate how important it is to know "the story behind the story." Every passage of Scripture has a context in history, in the book in which the story appears, and in the Bible itself. Every story assumes that readers and hearers know this context. Of course, we don't live in Bible times, and we don't speak the languages of the Bible. We simply don't know what the first readers and hearers of Scripture knew. That is why study is so important. Hopefully *Wow! I Didn't Know* has motivated you to learn more about Scripture in its original settings and has shown you that learning more really isn't that difficult.

You can learn more by adding a few books to your personal library. Here are some books that will help you go deeper into the New Testament: We recommend the *Understanding the Bible Commentary Series* published by Baker Books. The commentaries are easy to read and are designed for non-experts. Craig Evans wrote the commentary on the Gospel of Luke (1990/2011) in this series. Another set of commentaries that you will find very helpful is the *For Everyone* series by Tom Wright, the well-known British New Testament scholar and popular speaker, published by Westminster John Knox Press. They are short, easy to read, and to the point.

If you wonder about some of the crazy stuff about Jesus in popular media, you will want to look at Craig Evans's *Fabricating Jesus: How Modern Scholars Distort the Gospels* (InterVarsity Press, 2006). If you want to be blessed, you will enjoy his *What Grace Is: Meditations on the Mercy of Our God* (Lexham Press, 2022). You can visit Craig's website for more resources: craigaevans.com or watch his many YouTube videos at @CraigAEvansHCU.

Dear Friend,

This book was prayerfully crafted with you, the reader, in mind. Every word, every sentence, every page was thoughtfully written, designed, and packaged to encourage you—right where you are this very moment. At DaySpring, our vision is to see every person experience the life-changing message of God's love. So, as we worked through rough drafts, design changes, edits, and details, we prayed for you to deeply experience His unfailing love, indescribable peace, and pure joy. It is our sincere hope that through these Truth-filled pages your heart will be blessed, knowing that God cares about you—your desires and disappointments, your challenges and dreams.

He knows. He cares. He loves you unconditionally.

BLESSINGS!
THE DAYSPRING BOOK TEAM

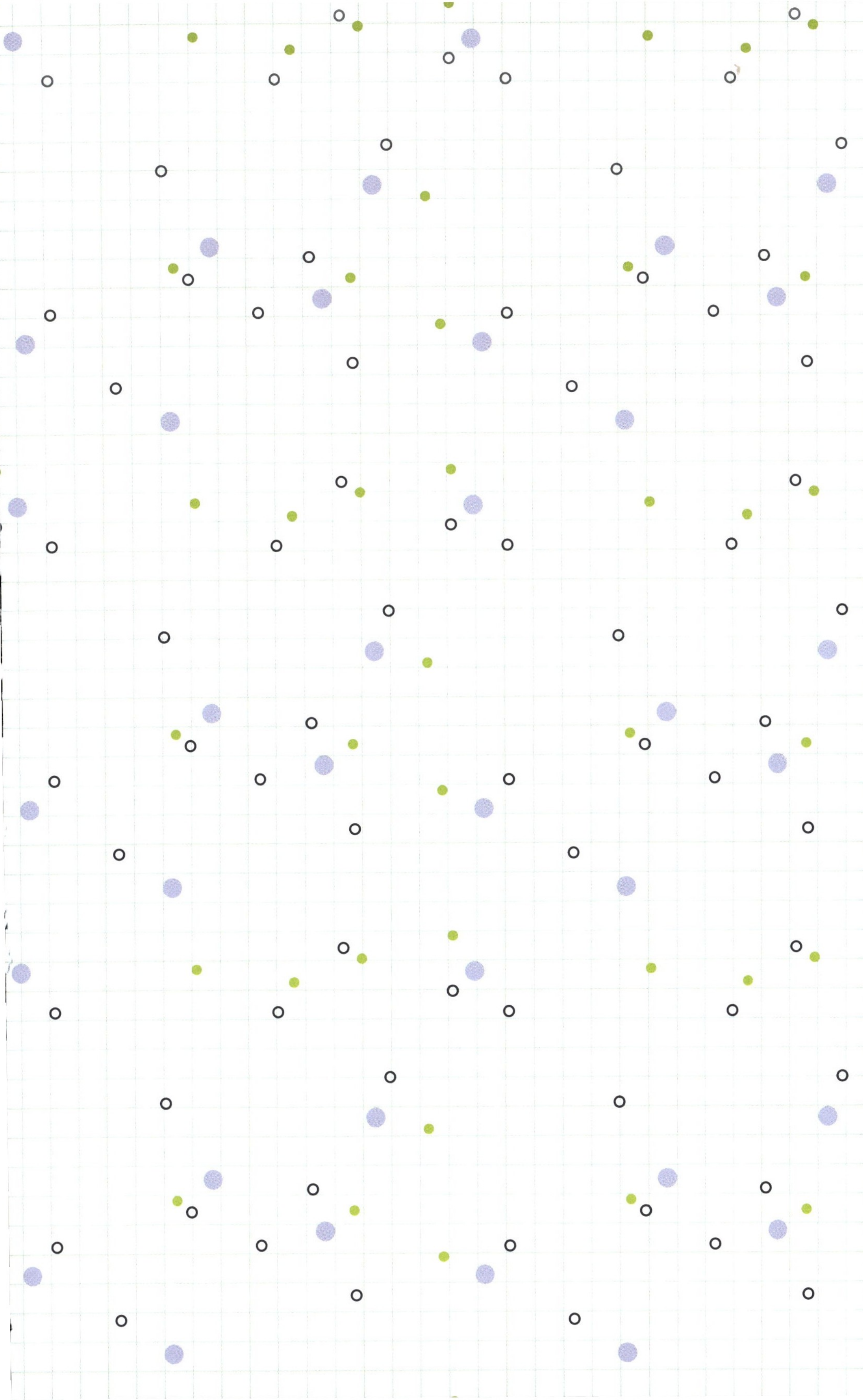

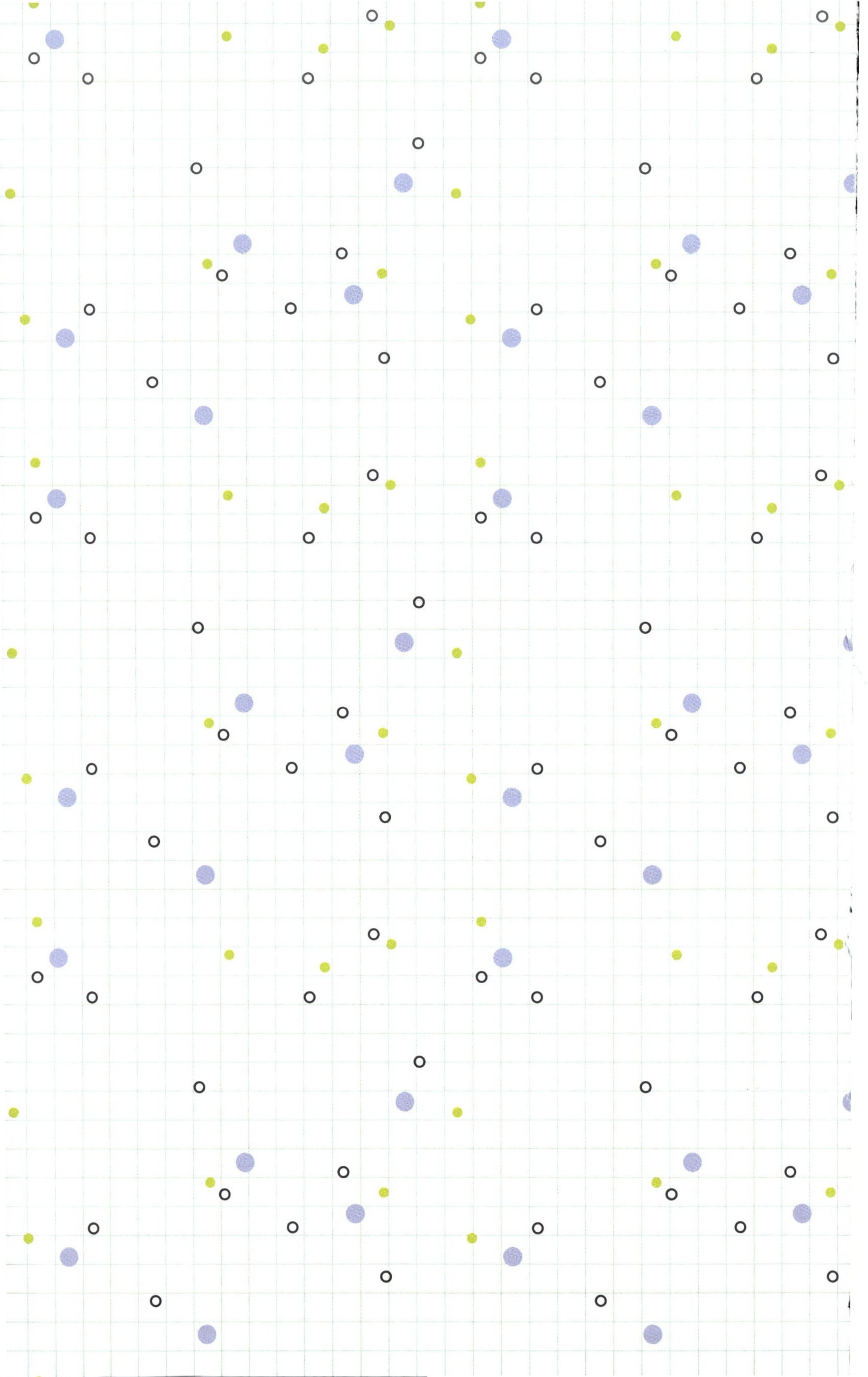